For the patients and staff in hospitals across Edinburgh and the Lothians who embraced Functionsuite with imagination and foresight, supporting new, uncharted creative relationships.

EXTRAORDINARY EVERYDAY

EXPLORATIONS IN COLLABORATIVE ART IN HEALTHCARE

Artlink Edinburgh & the Lothians

Preface
Caz McIntee

This book presents fourteen collaborative art projects that took place in hospitals across Edinburgh and the Lothians between 2003 and 2005. The aim of Functionsuite was to establish and extend creative relationships between artists and members of the hospital community. The aim was not to make art about or for the community: it was to make art with the community.

Thus began a series of conversations, relationships, and complex communications about contemporary art. A remarkably diverse network of people participated, including cleaners, ambulance drivers, switchboard operators, patients and ex-patients, managers, scriptwriters, porters, nurses, doctors, actors, architects, neurologists, self-help groups, play workers, and children as young as six. In some cases, the artists met with their collaborators just a few times; in others, contact was sustained for over two years. The number of collaborators in each project ranged from just two to hundreds.

This book aims to examine the complexity of these relationships and the works that emerged.

With the collaborative process taking centre stage, social anthropologist Justin Kenrick joined the project at the outset to study relationships as they developed. His contribution to this book raises questions both about the specific collaborations and about the project's overall relationship to society. In order to examine the process from different perspectives, three essays were commissioned while the collaborations were still in progress. One of these writers might have dipped into a project when it was going well; another might have visited during a more difficult phase. The timing of their visits allowed them to reflect on the creative relationships as much as the outcomes. Artist and writer John Beagles, journalist Magnus Linklater, and Artlink's

Some of the Functionsuite artists, staff, volunteers, collaborators and participants outside the Functionsuite hut at the Royal Edinburgh Hospital. July 2005

projects director Alison Stirling have each provided insightful texts that explore the limits, achievements and difficulties of the collaborations.

The experience of the hospital community is represented in the introduction, in which anaesthetist Dr David Wright reflects on his involvement in the project entitled A Paper Marriage. And clinical development nurse Sue Robertson and commissioning nurse Susan Tennyson – contributors to ...and the trainees, ARoundhead and The Ideal Ward projects – lead a discussion with core Functionsuite artists Kate Gray and Anne Elliot.

Most of the space in this book is given to the projects themselves. Many of them culminated in a finished artwork, public event or presentation, but for those that did not, where process remained the central concern, their appearance in this publication takes the place of presentation at a physical location.

Finally, Artlink director Jan-Bert van den Berg has contributed an afterword that discusses the organisation's approach to the project, and ponders on what lessons have been learned.

Collaborators, artists, organisers and writers explore and question the relationships and results. Our aim is to give you, the reader, access to the perspectives, processes and artworks, which we hope will inspire your own questions and ideas, and widen the on-going conversation about collaborative art practice. ■

Texts

Projects

Introduction
Dr David Wright

I have been asked to give a personal view of Functionsuite from the perspective of someone working in a hospital. There is a certain logic in this, as for the last few years I have enjoyed working with Artlink in their efforts to bring art into the hospital environment and I am involved in one of the current Functionsuite projects. But writing about the projects rather than responding to an artist's questions is a rather different matter. How and where should I start?

When faced with such tasks, what I normally do is to look for some background information, then allow a time for processing, before putting down some thoughts. These preliminary musings then generate other ideas and after a while I find myself with a structure and something to write about.

My most instructive background reading came from the Functionsuite website www.functionsuite.com. This contained, among many other things, observations from Justin Kenrick, the lecturer from Glasgow University who has been providing a social anthropologist's overview of the project. He emphasises that anthropologists try to see the world from the point of view of the group of people with whom they are working. He cites the example of the Mbuti people from Central Africa and what he calls demand-sharing, where those who have an excess of anything are liable to be asked to share it with those who have less. When this philosophy is applied to the Functionsuite projects, there should be mutual sharing between artist and collaborator which may lead to real co-ownership.

Having considered these thoughts, I felt it might be helpful for me to think what an ideal Functionsuite project might be and then compare that with my experience of working with Anne Elliot. Firstly the project should be truly collaborative, clearly formed from elements that have come both from the hospital community in

Project: A Paper Marriage

Paper marriage is a beekeeping technique used when two colonies of bees are to be united in one hive. Sheets of newspaper in which small holes have been made are placed between the two boxes which hold the colonies. The bees enlarge the holes, but this takes time, during which the bees are able to get used to each other, thus allowing the two colonies to be safely united.
– Dr David Wright

some way, as well as from the artist. Next, it should have a useful impact on the hospital community, perhaps by making people think about issues that they might not have otherwise considered, perhaps by changing attitudes in a positive way. Ideally, the wider that impact and the more helpful its effect on the community, the better. Finally, it helps if the project facilitates the progress that Artlink is making in engaging with the hospital community, rather than making this progress less likely to occur, that is it should produce a switch-on rather than a switch-off effect.

With these thoughts to go on, how do I view my working with Anne Elliot? Anne wanted to look at my interest in beekeeping and contrast it with the professional life of an anaesthetist, working in intensive care. My hospital life has been busy, working often at night and weekends and it has been emotionally demanding, with tragic deaths and miraculous recoveries. Out-of-hospital activities, such as walking, gardening and beekeeping, play a vital restoring and supporting role to balance these pressures . Anne started with an email questionnaire and then followed this with interviews, combined with visits to watch beehives being opened in the garden. This allowed her to video hive examination and handling of bees. She also took part in the extraction of honey by spinning it from combs and she watched its subsequent filtering and storing. From this she made a preliminary video, which we watched and then discussed. The discussions were aimed at editing the videoed material, with the intention of producing what we thought were the most interesting and useful images. We agreed that we

Dr David Wright was a consultant anaesthetist for 25 years at the Western General Hospital in Edinburgh, until his retirement this year. A major part of his professional life has involved working in intensive care, and interests in art and beekeeping have provided rewardingly different perspectives.

wanted to emphasise the pleasure that resulted from beekeeping, but because beekeeping has a very definite discipline, we felt that it had to be done in a logical way. This would lead from the development of bees in the hive to collection of nectar and pollen and then from the beekeeper's harvesting of honey to the exhibition of honey and wax at shows. There was discussion about whether it would be a good or bad thing to show long clips of repetitive manoeuvres. We talked of more footage of bees foraging on summer flowers and of trying to get some footage of swarming in early summer, recognising the inherent unpredictability of this. I was given a clear feeling by Anne that the eventual outcome would be something that we had agreed on together, even if this took longer than was originally planned.

How does this compare with my ideals for a project, described above? The issue of appropriate collaboration was carefully considered throughout by Anne. She has seemed to enjoy our involvement. I certainly derived great pleasure and satisfaction from showing her things and explaining what we did. Although an important aspect of the project, its resultant impact on others, cannot be assessed until there is an opportunity to see what is finally produced. It is useful to examine what effect it has had on Anne and me. Anne seems ever-positive and comes up with useful ideas each time we meet. I have had to think about what we could do and how best we might achieve it. This has changed as we've progressed and bounced ideas off each other. We have thought about how we can compare my busy life in hospital – its focus,

Anne Elliot: What do you know about the special properties of honey?

Dr David Wright: I have several books devoted to this. There are antibiotics in honey and consistent evidence that wound healing is helped by the application of honey.

order, safety consciousness, discipline and planning – with my beekeeping and the life of the bees.

What conclusions can I draw? Being asked to consider my thoughts for a foreword has been most helpful. As well as reminding me of how Functionsuite has come about, it has taken me to the Functionsuite website and given me a broader view of the project. It has, in particular, allowed me to be aware of Justin Kenrick's emphasis, as an anthropologist, on the importance of seeing other people's point of view and the concept of demand-sharing. By this, I mean understanding that those who have should recognise their good fortune and see it as a responsibility to share with those who have not. In a more focused sense, it will encourage me to think again about how we can complete something about beekeeping, which really changes people's lives. This may come through making them aware of the pleasures of beekeeping, or from helping to bring a deeper insight into relationships, whether with other humans or with other creatures.

The Functionsuite projects show not only how valuable the iterative process can be, where ideas are repeatedly considered, modified and reconsidered until an optimal endpoint is reached, but also that by giving to others you may gain a usefully different perspective. ■

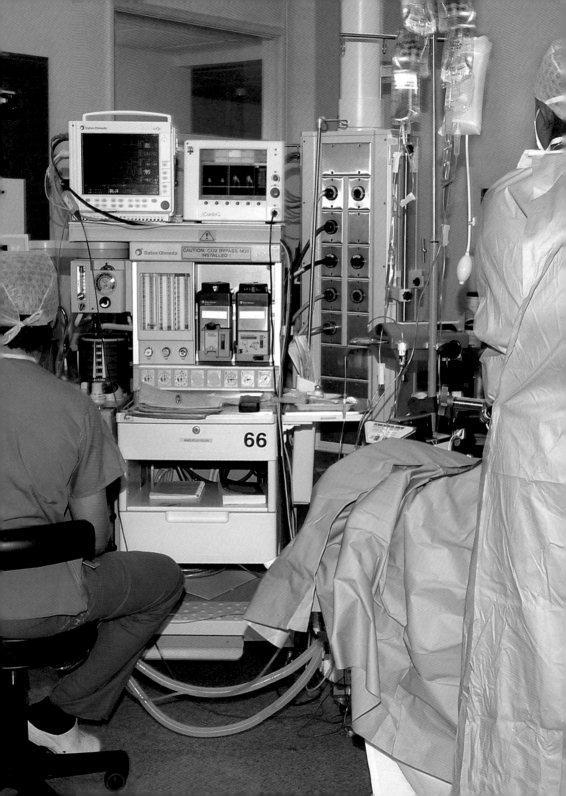

Alexander Donald
Building ↑

Is Collaboration the Cure?

Justin Kenrick

At my first real meeting with Kate, Anne and Caz – the Functionsuite team – we discussed the potentials and pitfalls of artists collaborating with patients and staff. How can artists work in a hospital context in a project that will constantly challenge them to be collaborative? Is true collaboration possible, collaboration that doesn't involve appropriating the experiences of others?

Another time, when we were joined by Alison Stirling, Artlink projects director, we talked about the discussions in which all of the artists' ideas for collaborative projects were held up to scrutiny by Functionsuite and Artlink managers as well as by myself. Is Fuctionsuite's work about controlling artists' ideas and controlling their 'making'? Or is it about trying to shift our understanding of what is going on in any creative 'making'?

> Caz: *We are asking people [the artists] to expose themselves when they are very raw (when they haven't yet fully worked out their ideas about what they might do, and haven't spent time in the hospital) so trust has to be equal in the whole group.*
> Alison: *Here artists are expected to change their minds constantly. Normally artists' ideas are sacrosanct, they are not used to being challenged, and so can easily feel insecure here.*

In a society that forces competitiveness and sees only individual achievement, the nature of creativity is concealed. As a consequence of my work as a social anthropologist, I believe that creativity is always relational – always emerges out of the interaction between people, and between people and particular environments. In a collaborative project such as this, artists are encouraged to remain open to the equal importance of diverse contributors. But even remaining open to such processes can be frustrating for people more used to focusing on making:

Project: Mimic Me

Stewart Murray and I talked about watching actors on television playing what start to seem like 'real' people – and about how, over time, we might confuse an actor with the character he or she is playing. We wondered if something similar was happening within the psychiatric hospital.
– Anne Elliot, core Functionsuite artist

Artist (to Kate): *The one thing that puzzles me is that you are here as a visual artist so don't you want to do your visual artist thing?*
Kate: *In some ways I'm happy to...*
Artist: *You're an artist, don't you want to make something?*
Kate: *I like making things, but I also want to make something happen... I want to feel creative in this, but the outcomes change with all the conversations I am having, and I don't want to put a stop to that yet.*

Having long been involved in working collaboratively on arts projects in this hospital context, Kate and Anne were in a sense set up as experts in the area. Caz was brought in as project manager, running the complex site-specific situations, contracts and relationships. All three are artists, but in this project the process, the relationships, the management are perhaps the central 'making', rather than simply intense backstage work which enables some front-stage production.

Relationship is Everything: Mimic Me

Putting the relationship with the patients or staff centre stage, engaging with them while waiting to see what will emerge, requires enormous confidence. It can seem as though the artist is indecisive, because that is exactly what they are trying to be. Anne working with Stewart was exactly this, while they developed a whole range of creative possibilities, 'a plan together of things we could do'.

Working with the actors felt good. Sean Hay
impersonated me and so did Morna Burdon.
You always got feedback on what you were doing.
Seeing pictures of myself on video is strange
but good, it's got a positive message.
The main thing about it was making friends.
– Stewart Murray

Over time, she and Stewart worked out an idea that became two
actors mirroring Stewart and Anne on camera. It is a brilliant film
to watch. Stewart had normally seemed quiet and shy but here he
is absolutely confident and centre stage: Sean (an actor) imitating
or improvising in response to Stewart's movements, words,
rhythms – a dance of deepening appreciation. Anne seemed to
be much more self-conscious and uncomfortable on the screen.
Seeing her working with patients, it was clear that the ability to
relate, to live with uncertainty, to develop friendships, to be in
there for the long term, was key.

How much is placing patients and staff centre stage an example of
true collaboration, and how much does it enable Anne to avoid the
limelight herself? In the editing process, Anne managed to sideline
herself. Is this example the epitome of collaboration or is there
something missing? Is the artist's presence being appropriated and
sidelined by the artist herself? Is such a thing possible?

The contrast between this strongly collaborative process and
individual 'makings' was uncomfortable at times for me. Alan
Currall – a consultant to Stewart and Anne's video project – was
invited one afternoon to show his video work to patients and staff.
The brief video pieces were brilliant and disturbing: documenting
solo performances by the artist which reflected on the absence
of relationship and on male identity – something Anne was aware
Stewart was very interested in. One ex-patient commenting on a
clip said: 'I did the same thing but ended up in here'; he left the

Film that I'd Like to make with
Ann.

An idea for A film that I would like
to make with Stuart. What would
you like the film to be about?

I would like the film to be
dedicated to The patients.

Whose The star of the film?

Is it an actor that could play
the part of a real patient?
What is about the patients
you would like to highlight in
the film?

Its not about The patients, its only
dedicated to Them.

I would like to make a film in
which we work out the Ideas
together. I am interested in
                    portraiture.

Our perceptions as to who we really are and other people's perceptions of us are both dependent on our position in the hospital. What would happen if we blurred our understanding of ourselves and asked actors to play us? We decided to video the results and show the tapes in the hospital and the wider community.

– Anne Elliot, core Functionsuite artist

screening shortly afterwards. There was a strong contrast between these non-collaborative 'makings' and the collaborative context they were being shown in: the noise of people interacting behind the sliding doors in this Church Centre in the hospital grounds, and the single figure of the male artist and his voice both on the screen and commenting on his video work.

We are used to watching the TV or video screen as if we were merely passive consumers, when in fact watching involves our active creativity, our unstoppable sense making. This becomes obvious as my body shakes with laughter and my eyes open wide with amusement and amazement as I sit with Stewart watching him and Sean – one on each TV monitor – mimicking and dialoguing with each other.

>>

Stewart Murray: *What do you think of power?*

Sean Hay: *I think too few people have it, and the ones that do have it tend to misuse it.*

Stewart: *I agree with you.*

Sean: *What do you think is good about power?*

Stewart: *You need power to live.*

Sean: *Like a personal power, like an internal power, everyone should have power.*

Stewart: *Absolutely! Can we have a break?*

Stewart: *A sponge has lots of holes in it.*

Sean: *Like life.*

Sean: *Sponges are great things because they always go back to their original shape ... . I like the colour of the sponge.*

Stewart: *It goes with your shirt.*

Sean: *What does it look like against your shirt? You've got a sponge on your shoulder!*

Stewart: *Correct. Will we stop and have a break? Yeah, let's go out for a fag. You look like Sean Hay.*

Sean: *I am relieved.*

Sean: *[Off camera] Is there power in success do you think?*

Anne Elliot: *[to Morna Burdon] I have been thinking about whether there is power in success, what do you think?*

Morna Burdon: *I think there is enjoyment in success.*

Stewart: *[Off camera] Yeah, that's true.*

Morna: *What's your success?*

Stewart: *[Off camera] Lift your head up. That's better. I can see your face when you lift your head up. I can see it in full view of the camera.*

Anne: *Success... you have got your own measure of success, but usually it is when other people measure how successful you are. But I like to think I set my own goals...*

Morna: *I don't know you at all.*

Anne: *I don't think I know who I am. It would help sometimes. I have learned a lot more about myself since I turned 40.*

Morna: *Oh have you. So what have you learned about yourself?*

Anne: *I never thought I was perfect, but there is really nothing perfect about me at all!*

Morna: *Have you got a favourite imperfection?*

Anne: *It has been pointed out to me that I blank people. So if you were to say something like...*

Morna: *Hello ... I see what you mean.*

Anne: *Apparently it's a very annoying thing to do.*

Morna: *I think that's quite a good imperfection.*

Project: **The Ideal Ward**

The proposed site for the new Royal Edinburgh Hospital

>> Shock and/or: The Ideal Ward

This particular project involved a series of focus groups that Steve Duval ran with ex-patients and staff, seeking to collectively imagine an ideal psychiatric ward which could potentially feed into the plans for a new hospital. I took part in several of the meetings and found the discussions often difficult, but fascinating.

Attendance fluctuated but patients and staff kept coming back. Steve had a strong agenda, seeking to highlight the barbaric history of mental health institutions and hoping that imaginative ideas could contribute to a different experience. He was hoping the patients would challenge the institutions, whereas their focus was more on wanting to be treated humanly. The patients' focus was on the place being homely, comfortable, with good food, massage not drugs, and there being consideration of others: 'if you're not well then you need to be encouraged ... take your mind off things and learn something constructive ... you need to build up relationships.'

The dynamics in the group could be difficult and Steve's interventions often led to illuminating contributions, such as when he suggested integrating the hospital into the wider society. One member of staff was aghast at the idea of coming to live full-time in the way patients do. This nurse also felt that the place should not be too 'ideal', that it shouldn't be too pleasant or people will want to stay. But it was Steve's statement (as part of his brief history of mental hospitals) that 'until recently this hospital had still

The group discarded the sixties' Utopian ideas about
mental health care that I had brought with me.
They simply wanted a more relaxed and supportive
environment and my assumptions about the need
for radical change were necessarily blown apart.
– Steve Duval, artist

carried out the barbaric practice of ECT[1]' that drew the strongest response from staff, who pointed out that it was still used here and could be a very helpful intervention. This in turn drew a response from some ex-patients who were strongly against the use of ECT, while others were less certain. Steve and I had passed the sign for the ECT ward every time we entered the Functionsuite office: what caused us both to remain blind to the obvious here and so see a complex situation in black and white?

Steve's project came in for much criticism in the Functionsuite meetings. The idea of creating a brief for an ideal ward seemed too awkward and simplistic, and building in collaboration through focus groups seemed to be too inflexible. But Steve said: 'I'm trying to make an object/tool and want to see how they'll use it. Will they be responsible to each other?' He added: 'I do want control though.' He wanted a degree of control in the midst of difficult discussion in order 'to make it safe for nurses and patients to say what they want to say'.

Did this control make for safety or for a lack of listening? Patients did not seek to create a radical 'non-institution', but instead focused on wanting comfort and friendship, and on wanting 'patients to be allocated to psychotherapists who show empathy towards them'. However, these wishes need not be understood as colluding with a conventional and oppressive institution (as Steve and I appeared to see them) but as being about emphasising human relationships.

What I think we were being asked to do is think of an ideal ward, but without thinking about the realities of mental illness and behaviours driven by mental illness – but what would be the point of that? What would be the point of having an ideal ward that we could never use?

It would not be a ward at all.

– Susan Tennyson, commissioning nurse

My sense was that the process needed less background information on institutions and more space to foreground participants' actual experiences. To focus less on an ideal ward and more (as was suggested in one of the meetings) on 'What's the ideal way to get better?' Steve sought an ideal, staff and patients reacted to this. But so did the rest of us in the Functionsuite meetings that focused on Steve's project.

Anne: *We wanted to support and challenge Steve to be flexible but we didn't inspire him to change, so he didn't inspire his group to change. He had a fixed idea of the ways in which he wanted the patients to be flexible, but we had a fixed idea of the ways we wanted him to be flexible.*

If we had focused more on really listening to Steve's experience, then it seems very likely that the focus groups might have taken a different tack: opening up rather than shutting down the dynamic patterns and processes of lived experience.

>>

the brief
The Ideal Ward Brief

Introduction to the brief
This brief has been drawn up without financial or governmental constraints, and
users' needs have been prioritised. One ward has been designed, plus the facilities
the group felt were needed for it. Our intention is not to suggest that the NHS should
build the ward, but to propose what users of the facility would ideally like.

Elements that are a given
We assume that everyone at the hospital is either trying to get well or helping others
to get well; that there is consideration for others, be they patients or staff; that
decisions on the ward will be made on a consensual basis, unless medical reasons
dictate otherwise.

Logistics of the space
The ward should house no more than 20 patients, and there should be a minimum of
10 staff members. Each patient's room should be able to accommodate two people
but one person would live there; it should have a telephone and the patient should
have control over things like light and sound. The building would be on the outskirts
of the community in a semi-rural setting with easy access to public transport.
The grounds should be secure.

Recreational facilities
The building would house a small cinema, a library, a café, a massage/relaxation
therapy unit, an art gallery, and exercise and kitchen facilities. There would be three
distinct communal spaces for patients, each designed to have different amounts of

I expected there would be more opportunities to have a creative input by making drawings etc., rather than the conversation-based sessions. I felt these mirrored too closely the planning meetings the Patients' Council had already been involved in. There was repetition – like talking about how much space each patient will have.
– Ruth Rooney, project worker at the Patients' Council and focus group member

stimulus (sound, visual and social). One space should have a number of tranquil spaces (window alcoves etc.). The grounds outside should house a garden with a greenhouse and a small farm. There should be a forest with paths.

Activities
There are to be cooking, art, exercise, gardening and farming activities. Professionals in each field who have some training in mental health issues will run these facilities. The facilities will be accessible to patients during normal business hours.

Medical facilities
There should be spaces for individual consultation with psychiatrists, psychologists, pharmacists, physical therapists and nutritionists.

The feel of the space
We would like the space to feel homely, spacious, non-institutional, light, clean, modern, comfortable and flexible. The space should have a clear logic to it so that it is easy to use. There should be lots of plants, and furniture should be difficult to move about. There should be positive decorative art with a leaning toward landscapes.

Needs of staff
There should be a space available for staff to relax and keep their things. Staff should have access to all in-house facilities. There should be a day-care centre for children of the staff.

The Ideal Ward
The artist's perspective
Steve Duval

What I hoped to do was facilitate a discussion between nurses and ex-patients about their environment at the Royal Edinburgh Hospital. This, I hoped, would lead to the possibility of drawing up a brief for an ideal mental health ward. Forming the focus group within the disparate communities of the hospital was going to be difficult, but I felt that people were likely to be interested in the subject. The group that came together was made up of three ex-patients, the Head of the Patients' Council, and the Commissioning Nurse for the new Royal Edinburgh Hospital, who had previously worked in the wards. It soon became clear that much of the group's discussion was going to be based upon interpersonal relationships that had existed long before this project had started. The relationship between the members of the group was at times tense. This dynamic became the source of many disagreements and threatened the participation of members in the group. Fortunately nobody left for this reason.

The participants discussed their feelings about the existing buildings and the problems and successes of the current situation. I talked with them about the history of the mental health institution and how previous models have led up to the current one. We also discussed alternative approaches from the past like Pinel's[1] ideas about moral therapy, Erving Goffman's notion of the 'total institution'[2] and Kingsley Hall.[3] Laing's theories gave rise to a heated discussion – which was, in my opinion, surprisingly invested in the current system.

The paradigm shift that I had thought would be inevitable was not going to happen. I had been convinced that if I presented the group with alternatives to an institution that I perceive to be oppressive and antithetical to the healing process, the participants would create a completely new institution. I was very wrong. Over the weeks every alternative was discarded as being a bit too unconventional. What became apparent was the desire to subscribe to the norm. How can a society or institution accept you if you don't sign up to its version of healing? Of course there were complaints, but most of these were about the lack of resources and personnel.

In the end, the group's brief for the ideal ward resembled a retreat for over-worked executives in need of a relaxing holiday. The group discarded the sixties' Utopian ideas about mental health care that I had brought with me. They simply wanted a more relaxed and supportive environment and my assumptions about the need for radical change were necessarily blown apart. I had spent eight months researching the history and theory of mental health institutions. If I had surrounded myself with people who thought as I did, we would have come up with a very different model that fitted with the theories I had read. Thankfully, I didn't work with like-minded people and the brief for the ideal ward that we came up with is representative of what the focus group members wanted.

In every decision that we made, we tried to consider everyone in the hospital. In common with many previous designers of institutions, we found that drawing up a brief for a space that suited everyone led to it being a bit bland; we also concluded that neutral colours are good for people who are very sensitive to their surroundings. These discoveries don't jive with artistic principles of stimulation and questioning, but they explain exactly why these qualities are not found in mental health hospitals.

We wanted people in our ideal ward to create their own sense of space. Our brief gives patients privacy as defined by the environmental psychologist Irwin Altman, who described it as 'selective control to access of the self'.[4]

I found working within the context of the hospital the hardest part of the project. The institution is unquestioned by the mental health community that it serves, and the act of questioning it without being a member of that community is perceived as threatening and unjustified. I thought it was perfectly clear that 'total institutions' like the Royal Ed need to be re-invented, and my original hope in creating a brief for an ideal ward with a group of patients and staff from the hospital was that this would open up a discussion about this re-invention, but this did not happen. However, I learned a lot from the people I worked with about the difficulty of navigating your way through an illness.

Project: The New Republic

During four two-hour Sunday workshops, the children designed structures that they considered to be ideal, through the creation of stories, paintings and sculptural maquettes.

>> Revolution in the Revolution

The New Republic project focused on a locked courtyard in St John's Hospital that is overlooked by a few corridors and the children's ward: it is an inaccessible sloping wilderness overgrown with trees and shrubs. This is the place Paul Carter wanted to transform through encouraging the children in the ward to come up with plans for a utopia, which would then be translated into a miniature world in the courtyard. Access would probably not be possible, but then 'the idea of utopia as a place that can never be entered would be strengthened'. Paul proposed that it could be screened off: invisible, except from the balcony of the children's ward, making 'The New Republic in some ways exclusive to the children'. Following children's ideas 'to the letter' and visually excluding others, were both attempts to realise the 'potential for children to take control of the courtyard'. Paul didn't reckon for the revolution in the revolution.

He brought in Beth Cross, a storyteller, and she told the kids an elaborate Celtic creation myth. Listening to it, Paul thought they'd be bored, but they were enthralled:

Beth: *The story is in their eyes. I tell details that weren't in the original story but that I see in their eyes. What will catch and what won't? The kids carried the story into drawings and models of the imaginary world they wanted to create. It involved animals, 1050 wolves, and Disney characters, and the design moved towards a*

The children wrote a creation myth for their new republic, featuring fantastic animals who discover a new place at the centre of a forest and begin a new settlement. They also painted pictures of the characters to illustrate the story.

OUR TREEHOUSE ADVENTURE
The New Republic Creation Myth
(excerpt)

They all shouted with delight: 'We're flying!' Up they swooshed above the treetops.

Snowy swept his arm, pointing towards a high hill at the centre of the forest where the trees stood apart, spreading their great arms in wide arcs. At once the group sped towards them over the tousled heads of all the other trees. Soon they were circling round the sunny clearing, lower and lower until their feet lightly touched down near the largest tree of all.

Snowy said, 'You will be safe here, and are free to make it your home as long as you like. It is full of good make-believe just waiting for someone to make something good with it!'

Q. What did you like about the workshop?

A. You were able to express yourself freely.
You could let your mind wander.
– Simon McHarg, aged 13

Jamaican beach hut at night. What they wanted was not some miniature out-of-reach utopia, not a glimpse of a new republic, but a real outpost they could access. One kid said they wouldn't go in until there was access for the disabled.

Later – in my only direct involvement in the project – Paul, Anne and I drove out to St John's to a meeting with Bill Mooney from estates and Lynn Haddow and Mary Benson from the children's ward. We passed through dull monotonous corridors to reach the meeting in the locked ward:

Paul: *The kids in the workshops seemed to be deliberately misunderstanding me: wanting a structure, wanting access. I wanted to cut the trees back; the kids wanted a welcome to the jungle!*
Bill: *I had thought the idea was to make the courtyard a visual focal point that wouldn't have access?*
Lynn: *But then the kids took over the workshop!*
Mary: *It was young Simon who wanted to make sure that his disabled sister would be able to get out there.*
Bill: *The original idea would be great. Of all the courtyards in the hospital this is the worst one in terms of the practicalities of access.*
Mary: *That Sunday, I was fair chuffed with the kids' suggestions. Ultimately the question of access became more important, since the balcony (from which the kids would have viewed it) became part of someone's office and so no longer accessible for the kids.*

>>

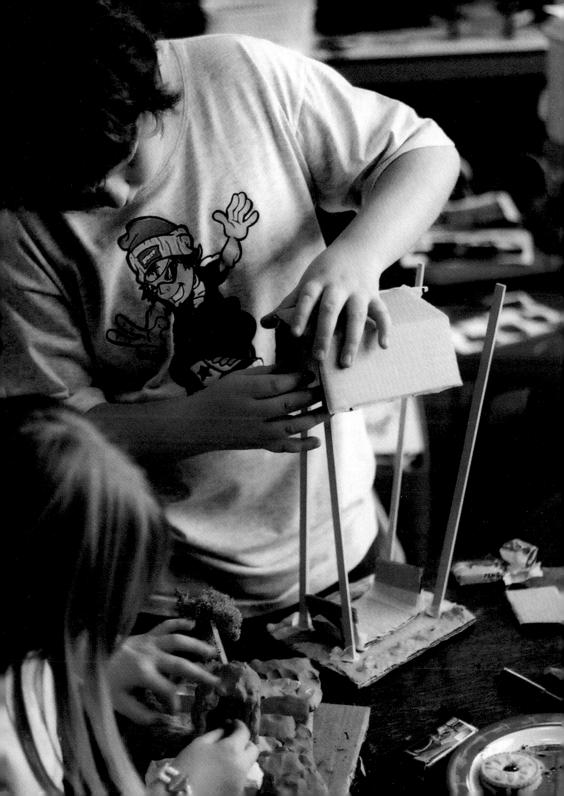

What has surprised me is that the project has
continued to develop, invoking many different
comments and opinions throughout the hospital.
– Lynn Haddow, ward charge nurse

>> *Now there is no general visual access for children if all the kids'
rooms on the courtyard side are occupied.*

Leaving these difficulties to one side, Paul had found a context for
dynamic and fruitful dialogue, and created a space (workshops) to
allow collaborators' imaginations to fire and redirect the project,
and space (meetings) to negotiate the possibilities. The process
involved enabling creative power, changing direction, and curbing
forces of control. In its context – and despite, or because of, the
tensions in the project – the process helped momentarily undo our
culture's Catch 22 function. This function continuously splits our
experience and the world into the active and the passive, the haves
and have-nots. It tells the have-nots that we are powerless, that
we can't do art, tell stories, shape life – that we can only watch. It
tells the haves that our worth comes from our power, our money,
our artistic genius, our whatever – that we mustn't acknowledge
equality. Both act as traps that cut us off from our ability to relate
creatively. Perhaps undoing this Catch 22 requires such revolutions
in revolutions.

>>

Project: Untold Tales of the Unexpected

Dr Adam Zeman takes a look at the 'Electrical Storm, Sketch 1' by Kate Gray, Functionsuite artist. The fishbowl and built in storm was put together by Kate as a visual metaphor expressing the effect of a seizure.

>> Who are we? Untold Tales of the Unexpected

Through discussing epilepsy and consciousness with Adam Zeman – a consultant neurologist at the Western General Hospital – Kate created the Electrical Storm. The piece was called 'Sketch 1' to emphasise that it was not a finished piece but part of a conversation. This artwork was her interpretation of a metaphor Adam had used to describe a certain sort of seizure. In a strange reversal of more normal approaches, the project started with a product, an artwork that emerged out of a sci–art dialogue, which was used to enable a process.

The project involved Kate exploring metaphors to describe the experience of epilepsy, and exploring the idea of epilepsy as a metaphor for our fear of loss of control. There was a real tension for Kate because, while epilepsy appears to be a surprisingly accurate metaphor for our general condition, it is also a real medical condition. This was evident when Adam suggested she show her artwork to an Enlighten epilepsy support group, but too many were strobe sensitive so she couldn't do this. She described her project instead, and they talked mostly of loss of control and fear, but few could think explicitly about metaphors. Her plan to get people to describe seizures or auras (pre-seizure feelings), to provide a bank of metaphors for people to draw on (ones that were not necessarily medical or mechanical), seemed to be coming unstuck. Adam pointed out that many of the metaphors Kate did gather were mechanical and technological (cars whose pedals do

hands tingle

Untold Tales of the Unexpected, Sketch 2

not respond, hard disks crashing, film projectors slowing to a stop
and speeding up) while others were experiential (being pecked
by a dead hen on a bed of straw, drinking lard and blood out of a
beaker).

Kate pointed out that if your mind is seen as responsible for your
own lack of control you are sent to psychology, but if your body is
seen as responsible you are sent to neurology. Adam mentioned
that even though most people diagnosed as epileptic don't have
epilepsy, the drugs can still work on them. So does the body/mind
split make much sense in this context? This was one of the projects
I was most intimately involved in, perhaps because it focused so
clearly on the problem of dualism and the question of who we really
are.

If epilepsy is about absence, then this write-up provides an
absence, the voice of people with epilepsy is absent from it.
Instead, the metaphors and images that drew my attention were
not so much the striking ones Kate gathered from sufferers of
epilepsy, but those which emerged in conversation with Adam,
Kate, and Maureen [a poet and volunteer at the hospital].

Adam emphasised the individual's body (he is a neurologist) while
I emphasised the ecological and social networks in which we are
embodied (I am an anthropologist). Maureen referred to how a
physical explanation need not exclude an explanation people might
describe as spiritual:

STAGES OF A SEIZURE:
Aura- warning before seizure
Simple partial Seizure- involves
  part of the brain, does not
  affect conciousness
Complex partial seizure- involves
  part of the brain, does affect
  conciousness
Tonic Seizure- Causes Stiffening
  while concious
Tonic Clonic Seizure- loss of
  Conciousness, stiffening,
  jerking and falling.

Adam: *A novelist found seizures a window into a different world before discovering it was epilepsy – did that devalue it? ... Epilepsy marks you out, which is why Hippocrates called it 'The sacred disease'. A theologian believes that it gives her spiritual insights.*
Maureen: *You can't rule that out.*

Kate pointed out that a spiritual understanding can be interpreted as being in opposition and superior to the everyday, rather than illuminating the everyday:

Kate: *It doesn't have to be spiritual or sacred to be meaningful – spiritual or sacred seems to me to mean 'removed from everyday life'.*
Maureen: *For me sacred can mean a particular place that has meaning for you, a top of a particular hill for example. Sacred means that the place has deep significance.*
Kate: *I want to value the ordinary, the everyday.*

Are such alternative explanations of similar phenomena mutually exclusive or mutually enlightening?

Again, we see a Catch 22 playing out in our culture: where two perspectives – rather than being seen as potentially mutually enlightening – become opposed by the dualism we have been so deeply instructed in. But the paradox that both Maureen and Kate point to is perhaps the essence of all these projects: an attempt to refuse the empty promise of individual talent and achievement

SYNAESTHESIA IS:
a linking of the
senses
eg: seeing a smell,
smelling a colour...
Some believe it is due to
'cross wiring' between
areas of the brain
Theories link it to
Creativity and production of
Metaphor. More women and
left handers have it

and to instead remain open to uncertainty, collaboration, and the extraordinary nature of the everyday. If alienation is the illness, is collaboration the cure?

Collaboration and Creativity: juxtaposing humans

As Beth the storyteller said:

When people say 'I can't tell stories', I say 'I defy you to go the rest of the day without telling a story. If someone asks you how your day was say "No"'

Although celebrity art would persuade us otherwise, creativity is not a substance inhering in the made object or the making artist. Creativity is perhaps better understood as being stretched by the unexpected, being challenged to juxtapose and relate previously separate experiences, or to consider as separate those aspects we had always assumed entailed one another. Juxtaposing artists, patients and staff – and putting the making process on pause long enough to let something unexpected emerge out of the relationships between participants and their particular environments – was the purpose of the Functionsuite research process. Did it succeed? To the extent that we recognise both the continuity and the disjuncture between what was expected and what happened, it succeeded.

TONIC CLONIC SEIZURES CAN HAVE THE SAME ELECTRICAL PATTERN IN THE BRAIN AS E.C.T (electro-compulsive - therapy, used to treat psychiatric conditions

Collaboration and Compassion: back in hospital with the humans

It is strange to be back in the Western General Hospital, not as an anthropologist and researcher but as a patient. ... I sit up in bed with the drip dripping through the needle into the vein in my arm in this windowless ward where four of us lie. I felt terrible when I came in, that feeling of dread, no-one seemed to know what was wrong or why.

... Collaboration ... here it is in ward 43b where nurses and doctors from all over the world, where support staff and patients (mostly Scottish), play out an absence of being in roles, or interact in conscious awareness of each other's humanity and so create a shape-shifting community. This location may not be the ideal ward but it is never the ward that needs to be ideal: it is people's idealness that needs recognising. Those consultants and doctors who have been highly trained into a particular kind of relationship in which the personal is absent hardly get a taste of reality, of the humour, the pain, the people, the healing – the nurses and support staff who pause, the patients on pause, certainly do.

... The hospital is co-created by those here who care and whose care is revealed in the thousand tiny acts of compassion that make the world, that have made me healthy enough to get up from this seat – my medicines delivered by a compassionate Italian – and go home. What makes collaboration work? I wonder... ■

Untold tales of the unexpected

meet Dr Zeman in his office after contacting general 'research groups' through the hospital directories

Dr Zeman is a neurologist specialising in conciousness, memory and epilepsy

During a conversation he explains simple partial seizures to me
(they involve only part of the brain and do not affect conciousness)

I am struck by how many art postcards Dr Zeman has on his office pinboard

To process the information Dr Zeman tells me I find myself thinking of a quiet productive kitchen, but when I open one of the cupboards there is an electrical storm inside.

I decide to make this metaphore, as a 'sketch' to show at our next meeting

WHAT METAPHORS DO WE USE FOR LOSS OF CONTROL IN MODERN SOCIETY?

Epilepsy is a state of electrical rebellion, in which the brain's electricity escapes its normal checks and balances and takes on a pulsating, synchronised life of its own. A focal seizure in the temporal lobe may cause an experience of déjà vu: in the occipital lobe, a hallucination of flashing lights; in the parietal lobe, an 'out-of-the-body' experience. During a focal seizure a 'double consciousness' often ensues, combining the abnormal experience induced by the seizure and a normal reflective awareness of events. Seizures can sometimes be induced by stimulation – flashing lights, a particular tune or even a certain thought – and can sometimes be resisted by a mental act, like intense concentration or an effort to relax.

Meetings with Kate, then Kate and Justin, and most recently Kate, Justin and Maureen, have been stimulating. Kate's installation, a medicine cabinet containing an artificial thunderstorm above a tangle of wires, was arresting. Justin brought an anthropologist's breadth of vision to my longstanding ruminations about mind and brain and Maureen contributed the poet's arresting concision. I am keen to see the fruits of Kate's final plan, which is to spend a few minutes supine in Princes Street, recreating the experience of someone recovering from a major seizure while filming the reactions of passers by from that low and vulnerable vantage point.

Dr Adam Zeman

I carry the box across the car park to the amusment of passers by

I ask dr Zeman if in his expevence people often used metaphor to descnbe seizure experiences

Dr Zeman Suggests I show the cupboard sketch to people who suffer seizures and see if they use metaphors.

I contact support groups and make arrangements to meet people confidentially.

As the cupboard contains strobe lighting many in the groups cannot look at it, but many descnbe seizures and auras to me

they suggest that I am interested in and use metaphor because I am an artist

6 meetings with groups and individuals

Many worry that thinking about seizures may induce one

In descriptions there are many metaphors. I collect them and ask to use them

List of Metaphors

Sitting in a cinema and the film begins to slow down until it stops. Then it begins again, slowly gaining speed.

Everything is spread out as if it is exploding.

I'm in a car but the brakes don't work.

Butterflies in my stomach.

There are stars and black floaters.

Stranded on a little island.

It's like voodoo.

I'm in a removed state, like dreaming. Some nice and some nasty.

Drinking lard and blood out of a beaker.

My brain has got lots of information... too much.

I feel as if I've run for miles

I fall on a bed of straw and a dead hen pecks me.

The postman delivers mail and puts it through the wrong door or it is lost in the post for a while.

It is a supernova going off across the cortex of the brain

Someone administering different amounts of electricity.

Hard disc has crashed... then reboots itself.

I'm in a car and the oil stops going through.

Someone has wiped me clean

The back of my brain is kicking.

Feel like I'm up in the sky looking down.

I take metaphors back to group which now includes Justin Kenrick (social Anthropologist)

We decide to also ask Doctors for metaphors. I have many meetings but only collect one "faulty car alarm"

I take maternity leave (twins!)

When I get back I meet Maureen Sangster, writer and poet. Maureen uses the collected metaphors as a starting point to make 6 poems

Justin Speaks about how metaphors "jump tracks"

We all meet together, talk about how different people interpret the same thing in different ways, Seizures.

Antropologist – other cultures interpret seizures as
* Entering conciousness of other realms
* Possesion
* Right of passage / Liminal

Doctor – a means of diagnosis, Unlocking doors to explain physical problems

Writer – * visionary   * personal communication
* Spiritual

Artist – Symbol of control / loss of, death and resurrection

*Conclude. Plan to make film looking up at the sky in a busy place, use metaphors as subtitles.

I fall on a bed of straw

d a dead hen pecks me

Delicate Territory

Magnus Linklater

Illness is an isolating process. I remember a dying friend asking me whether I had ever been seriously ill, and when I replied that I had not, he said: 'You cannot begin to understand the way that illness takes over your life. It dominates every hour of your waking day, it invades your dreams by night, it sets you apart from the rest of the world, because they are well and you are not.'

Thus, when Functionsuite argues that the hospital is a community, and seeks to establish a series of collaborative projects between the community and the artist, it is venturing onto delicate territory. What kind of a community is it that can draw together individuals caught up in their own world of sickness? What possible dialogue can the artist have with those whose principal interest is the process of their own recovery? And finally, how can the artist maintain the integrity of the creative process if the community becomes the dominant partner? Too much input from others, and the original concept may be swamped. Too little, and the whole purpose of interaction is lost.

The three Functionsuite projects that I examined have met these dilemmas head-on, with very different results. In all of them, the artists have sought to engage patients and staff in developing ideas whose outcome, by their very nature, could not be predicted. They believe that the process of collaboration has been critical to the success of each project. They regard the interaction between artist and participants as the defining aspect of their work. Above all, they have seen individuals drawn together and involved in something external which appears, nevertheless, to echo some aspect of their own intuition and imagination.

Paul Carter, who has been working on a project called The New Republic at St John's Hospital in Livingston, set out with some fairly clear, if unspecific, ideas of how it might turn out.

Paul Carter with nursing staff outside The New Republic

He believed that the concept of a new republic carried with it overtones of Conrad's Heart of Darkness, or William Golding's Lord of the Flies, both works in which remote groups of people break free of the holds of civilisation – for better or for worse. He wanted the young patients in the children's ward to come up with their idea of a perfect place to live, a place of escape, created by them, in their imagination. The hospital, an anonymous concrete and glass sprawl of buildings, offered a space which was in one way ideal, in another hopeless – a hemmed-in courtyard, overlooked by windows, with no access from either wards or corridors. Some bushes had been planted there and it was, as Carter called it, 'jungle'. He imagined that the children might want to create a mini-republic there, and envisaged a balcony, from which a Mussolini-style dictator would proclaim his new state.

The children in the ward had other ideas. They began to draw a retreat – a wooden stockade-type cabin, which would be the perfect bolt-hole, reached by a ramp, with a rough-and-ready door which could be pulled up to keep out intruders. Their drawings were amateurish, but definite, and Carter accepted them without question. 'I was determined to treat their amateurism as a level of professionalism,' he says. 'Their ideas would be obeyed to the letter because they were the clients – they were all-powerful.' The result is just as they imagined it – a little wooden hut, raised above the ground, a bit skew-whiff, but with a brightly painted roof, like something Robinson Crusoe might have knocked together on his desert island. In building it, Carter was careful not to make

Participant in a drawing workshop,
childrens ward, St John's Hospital as part of
The New Republic project.

something too professional. He likes the contrast between the
nailed-together spars and the steel and glass formality of the
hospital corridors.

Part of the project involves storyteller Beth Cross coming into
the ward and creating narratives linked to the project in the
courtyard. Since the children themselves had a hand in conceiving
the building, they find themselves totally involved. The fact that
it is inaccessible actually strengthens rather than weakens the
concept, in Carter's view. It is an imagined, unreachable place, and
the children understood this perfectly. They knew that they would
never be able to play there themselves, but thought that others
might do, some time in the future. 'By doing it for someone else,
they gained a sense of power,' says Carter. 'There is nothing more
powerful than doing something for other people.'

He concedes that his own ideas have been subservient to those
of the children, and goes so far as to admit that the submerging
of his own identity did at one stage concern him. However, it was
the total involvement of the participants that explains his ultimate
satisfaction with The New Republic. Although it has turned out very
differently from what he envisaged, he believes it is an expression
of Guy Debord's concept of the localised revolution.[1] 'This is the
revolution of the every day,' he says. 'It offers a disengagement
with society. It is doing something ambitious, but in an amateur
way. The thing may be small, but the idea is big.'

Project: Mayday Pavilion

The dome took one week to install with the Talamh Life Centre and a group of volunteers from Artlink.

The children's reaction was enthusiastic. One member of staff, who watched their participation said: 'I think story-telling played a large part in how they came up with their collective vision.' One of the participants commented: 'I like the literary references, and thoroughly enjoyed working on the project.'

Kate Gray's Mayday Pavilion in the Royal Edinburgh, a psychiatric hospital, is a similar exercise in contrasts. It sprang from widely discussed plans to build a new hospital. Everyone – patients and staff – had been talking about the new design, and what was needed. Meetings were arranged between Kate Gray, Albert Stewart Nicolson, a former patient with an interest in architecture and alternative therapies such as yoga, architect Paul Barham, and staff, to debate how these ideas might be realised, and what they thought about the non-clinical services offered by the hospital. Nicolson insisted that the Mayday Pavilion must be an inviting place, in contrast to many of the existing run-down wards. A questionnaire was brought to the meetings which asked people to design the kind of spaces they would like to see, and their views were recorded. A consultant was invited in, and Liza Fior, an architect from MUF[2], took part in a brain-storming exercise with staff and patients.

What emerged was the idea of a summer pavilion, built with material discarded by the hospital. 'We were using hospital waste to positive ends,' says Gray. People from the Talamh Life Centre in Lanarkshire, which practises environmental sustainability,

Events included cinema screenings (chosen through an open vote), tai chi, yoga and seated ballroom dancing (in which participants with mobility problems danced while sitting down, using arm movements). We also held a dinner on the last night, during which people from the hospital and interested parties from outside got together at a large table made up with hospital sheets and blankets to discuss what a hospital is or could be, and the role of art and artists in a social space.
– Kate Gray, core Functionsuite artist

were called in because the centre makes Buckminster Fuller-style geodesic domes. 'We thought it should be a dome,' added Gray, 'because most people's drawings were rounded and domed. Since Buckminster Fuller himself suffered from depression, we thought his ideas were in tune with the environment of a psychiatric hospital. The concept we came up with was very different from any idea I might have had at the start.'

Everything inside the chosen space is geared to sustainability. The parquet floor will be a 28-foot circle of recycled wood, the canopy will be of sheets made out of reconstituted wastage. Inside will be tables, which will be like beds, so that people can get into bed together while discussing their ideas. There are plans to involve patients in yoga, tai chi, knitting and ballroom dancing. Cycle generators will be available, to be used by patients for exercise, but which will also produce power for a small cinema. There will be a dinner, bringing all the participants and outside guests together.

The question that arises here is an intriguing one: where does therapy end and art begin? After all, one of the principal aims is to provide patients with activities which will enhance their sense of well-being. Gray is fairly convinced that the answer is: when the participants have control over the process. 'So often, the patients in hospitals like these aren't consulted. Seeing the process through from concept to completion, and knowing they have been involved in it from the start, justifies it as a project.

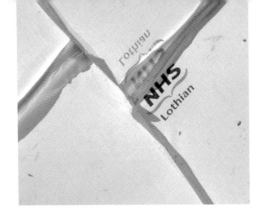

We were interested in creating an environment which was not part of the hospital but which commented on its structures. Made from the hospital's own waste, and situated within its grounds, it could act as a parasite. On the other hand, it could function as a self-contained unit, even generating its own power.
– Kate Gray

I feel it's jointly my work, and none of it would have happened without me – I'm the eye of the storm, if you like. But unless everyone had contributed, the project would not have had any validity. They've even voted on what films will be shown in the cinema – the first two are Carry On Doctor, of course, and Spider-Man 2.' Because the participants have been consulted at every stage of the process, with the artists in residence at the hospital for weeks on end, there is a sense of involvement in the end-product, even though not everyone was involved in the actual construction of the building. Again, the sense of artistic achievement stems from this active collaboration.

Nicolson came up with his own comments on the collaboration:

'Opening doors, as opposed to closing them to me, would be my appreciation of the Mayday Pavilion,' he wrote. *'I attended the yoga, tai chi, and the celebration meal, and found the venue inviting, calming, relaxing, delicious, and throughout of a standard which, if rolled out, would no doubt open avenues beyond the limited acceptance and capacities which inhibit and debilitate the experiential life of patients (i.e. sufferers of a psycho-socially induced condition.)'*

>>

Project: ARoundhead

Richard Wright of Mongrel lets loose the head and voice of Oliver Cromwell through the automated telephone system at the Royal Edinburgh Hospital. The ensuing phone calls encouraged staff to pass around messages, songs, jokes and rude noises.

>> Richard Wright and Graham Harwood of the Mongrel art team have taken a different route altogether. They are involved with the most ambitious, most complex, and ultimately least predictable of all the projects. The idea of ARoundhead has been conceived, specified and researched by the artists far more than the collaborators. Although its outcome depends ultimately on the active and willing participation of staff, their response is as yet untested, and there is therefore no means of knowing whether it will be a far-reaching success or a resounding flop.

The concept is a stylised one: at the Royal Edinburgh, the telephone system is an integral part of the hospital. However, with modern technology, it is possible to develop an additional telephone exchange which can be bolted onto it. Using this concept, the team intends to see how people within the hospital can be motivated to use this everyday system as part of an artistic project. It has therefore invented a story based on historical fact, but with a suitable degree of added fantasy: the head of Oliver Cromwell has been lost in the hospital's telephone system, and his disembodied voice from the 17th century will be calling up staff to test their response. Up to 200 phones will be involved over a three-week period.[3] The 'head' will communicate a series of messages using archaic English, in the hope of persuading the recipient to transfer the call to another patient or a member of staff. History is important to the project. The artists have researched the bizarre history of Cromwell's head – removed by royalists after his death and displayed on a pole outside Westminster Hall, then either lost

A script workshop led by David Griffiths is held to develop narrative ideas with hospital staff, and the scripts are written by Richard Wright. Eighteen final scripts are divided into two groups: individual 'functional' scripts which allow people to pass the head quickly on to another extension and a sequence of scripts which build up into a narrative.

or stolen; it was said to have been later bought, sold, displayed as a curiosity, then finally buried. Along the way it was said to have acquired talismanic powers – hence the idea of using it as a means of communication.

Problems have beset the project, as Richard Wright concedes. For a start, ARoundhead relies not only on sophisticated technology but on the active participation of hospital staff. Setting up conferences and meetings proved difficult, so that most of the preparatory work has been carried out without the collaboration on which it depends. Perhaps not surprisingly, the residents of the Royal Edinburgh have been less conversant with Cromwell's history than the artists might have supposed – and, given his malign reputation in Scotland, the head is not likely to elicit a warm response.

There will be a high proportion of baffled recipients, who know little about the project in advance of its going live, save that Cromwell's head will be calling them up and asking them to transfer his call.[4] 'People have no set idea of what is happening,' admits Wright. 'The head will be berating them, asking them questions, playing music, offering an apology, a joke, to see what they make of it. We will log which is the most successful and productive response, judged by whether they put the phone down, pass it on to another extension, or opt out altogether.' A script workshop run by scriptwriter David Griffiths was held at the hospital, and the artists have had a lot of fun with the dialogue.

[Project notes: Mongrel]

November 2004:
First job on site -> get ID – database is not connected to any other machine
-> so anyone who worked here in the past can have access to the building –
oh well, no one checks anything anyway. 4,000 standalone databases
– why?

Nip outside for a quick ciggy

I'm reliably informed by other people outside:

1
Beware of doctors! No begging for beer money!

2
Tie a silk scarf around your mouth and nose (e.g. soaked with
lemon), as soon as there is the threat of danger.

3
Gloves, change them when you enter the hospital, and clean them
inside/outside. Clean your hands, too.

4
Put a piece of copper metal (everybody has copper coins) in a bottle of
water, fill it up with water and leave it for one day; then take water
from there to clean (to wipe off) everything you or others have touched
before you cleaned your hands after having entered your home from
outside.

There are 800 end-point-users in the hospital telephone network
– pages of numbers, a lonely network of isolated form-fillers.
Bosses trying to gain info about workers' key strokes (keyboard
tagging) and tracking patients from entry into the system until
exit, amassing data for 'evidence-based practice' (what was it
before?). Hospitals run on security-conscious networks.

19 May – 2 June 2005:
the project takes place at the hospital.

When I received the first call, I just put the phone down. I thought it was a nuisance call that had somehow slipped through. I cottoned on after speaking to Teresa and then I enjoyed it, even though it was a bit weird. I passed it on to my supervisor who then passed it on to someone else. The girls I work with had a laugh – they thought it was funny.

– Helen Howell, member of staff at Royal Edinburgh Hospital

Sample extracts: *'If it pleases you to hear the head, then press the key that bears the symbol "one"...' 'Heed me gentle listener, for I have news that concerns you exceedingly. God has plucked your number out of obscurity ...' 'To claim your most happy reward you have but to press the key that bears the symbol "nine"...'*

The collaborative element of the ARoundhead project remains, therefore, to be tested. But the principle is consistent with the others. In each case, the artistic validity of the work depends on a two-way process. If the imagination and enthusiasm of those taking part is caught, then they succeed. If they turn out to be one-sided, they fail. That, it seems, is the definition of a Functionsuite project. There is no doubt that the collaborative element, when it takes off, can inspire both artist and participant. Above all, it produces surprises, and that is an essential ingredient of any worthwhile act of creativity. In the case of Mayday Pavilion and The New Republic the surprise has been a welcome one. In the case of ARoundhead, the jury is still out. Either way, however, Functionsuite is breaking new ground in defining the aims and direction of collaborative art. In doing so, it is involving a section of our society which all too often feels itself isolated from the rest of the world. If, by that means, it succeeds in creating a community where none existed before, drawing together individuals who may feel themselves detached by their illness, or rejected by an uncaring society outside the hospital walls, then it is achieving important results.

As to the dividing line between art and therapy, it can go hang. ◼

A Round head

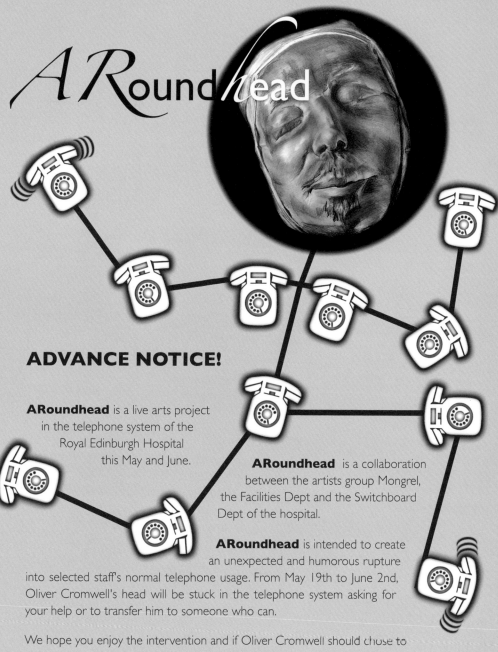

ADVANCE NOTICE!

ARoundhead is a live arts project in the telephone system of the Royal Edinburgh Hospital this May and June.

ARoundhead is a collaboration between the artists group Mongrel, the Facilities Dept and the Switchboard Dept of the hospital.

ARoundhead is intended to create an unexpected and humorous rupture into selected staff's normal telephone usage. From May 19th to June 2nd, Oliver Cromwell's head will be stuck in the telephone system asking for your help or to transfer him to someone who can.

We hope you enjoy the intervention and if Oliver Cromwell should chose to ring you, please spare a little time to hear him out or pass him around!

PLEASE EXPECT A CALL!

For more details on Functionsuite projects please visit : **www.functionsuite.com**

The head of Oliver Cromwell is stuck in the phone exchange of a psychiatric hospital.

A robot telephone system that interrogates the different departments and individuals. The robot will ring up and ask questions, record results, maybe creating conferencing networks between the various people it speaks to. Technically, Cromwell's head is a Linux-based computer plugged into the phone system. The head will dial a selection of the 800 staff phones at random. Over a number of days the strange phone calls from Oliver Cromwell's head will hopefully build into an urban myth. The project will be collaborative in that it will provide the staff with a means to interact with each other using the Cromwell character as a mediator. We will use the project to find out ways in which people can be motivated to communicate using a system like this.

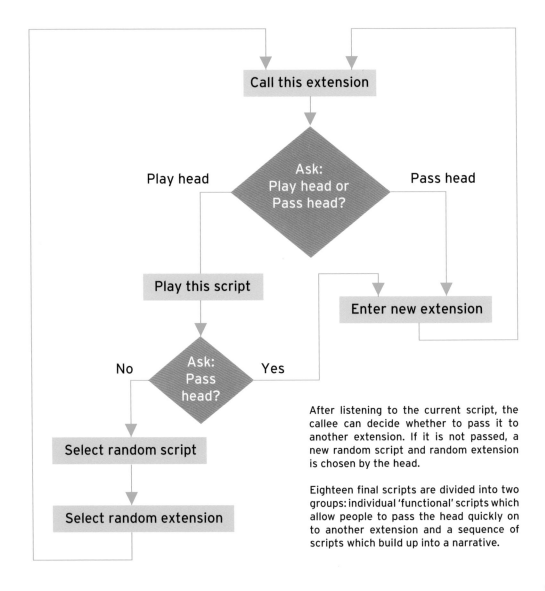

After listening to the current script, the callee can decide whether to pass it to another extension. If it is not passed, a new random script and random extension is chosen by the head.

Eighteen final scripts are divided into two groups: individual 'functional' scripts which allow people to pass the head quickly on to another extension and a sequence of scripts which build up into a narrative.

Sample narrative scripts_

> CROMWELL
Good person, I am in need of urgent release.
Centuries of bad air and rotten fumes have built
up inside me! I can hold it no longer ... ah ...

Loud fart noise.

> CROMWELL (continued)
Ah ... that is exceedingly refreshing. Perhaps you
can direct me to another line so I may release
more vapours? Pray enter an extension number
most speedily ... I feel another emission building
inside me ... <ext...>

Sample narrative scripts_

> CROMWELL
Where am I? Who is this at the end of this phone?
I remember descending into darkness. Nothing but
the rustling of seeds sprouting in the soil ...
daisies tickling my nostrils with their roots.

And now I find myself without a body, my head
ringing with the sound of wee gossiping voices,
whistling down thousands of little copper wires
in this hellhole called telephony!

If you know of another who can explain my
situation then press <one>. If you will allow me
to call upon you again then please press <two>.

Collaborators and Artists in Conversation

Sue Robertson, clinical development nurse
Susan Tennyson, commissioning nurse for the new Royal Edinburgh Hospital
Anne Elliot and **Kate Gray**, core Functionsuite artists

Meeting people and looking at art

SUE: Speaking as a layperson I find I can often understand the finished product but not the process. It's been great meeting people who are totally unencumbered by the medical model and have a fresh perspective on working with users of mental health services.

SUSAN: I would like to echo that. For me one of the huge successes in the Royal Edinburgh[1] has been the Artlink Gallery in the corridor. It allows you to meet people – patients, staff, visitors – in a context where you're not reacting in terms of any relationship other than as people looking at art.

SUE: I'd like to discuss how we could get staff in the hospital involved. We've gained so much, and there must be many other people who would enjoy the work and realise the importance of helping service users become involved in it.

SUSAN: It's not that people aren't interested but they may be reluctant to put themselves forward. People – the staff, for example – who put their work on show in the gallery must be reasonably confident that they have something to show in the first place. But there must be many people who are interested in what you're doing but have no thoughts of being any kind of artist and would never actually approach you. I'm talking about staff but it could be true for service users as well.

I think what's useful about the Artlink model is the way it is actually bedded in as a service that's integral to the hospital.

You need to show people the value of art, and that's what you're doing. For example, I would never have thought that something like the Mayday Pavilion[2] could be an art installation. I'm very concrete in my thinking.

KATE: With the Mayday Pavilion I'm really asking what art can do. I see the actual structure as very sculptural. You can also see it as art making a space for people to meet and talk about things.

SUE: I think the Mayday Pavilion was wonderful. But, Kate, how did you come up with the idea of using the waste products of an institution to make art? You know, all the old linen that's been used for years by many different people, hundreds if not thousands of times [laughter] ...it shows us different perspectives on waste and regeneration, making something good out of those big black skips overflowing with dirty linen...

ANNE: I suppose artists would look on anything as having potential.

SUSAN: The Pavilion made us start to think in a different way. If you had just described the project we might have rejected it, but once we actually saw it we realised its potential, and that made the next project less of a leap.

KATE: The idea of using waste products came out of lots of conversations, but also walking around with Albert[3] past the skips. Artists are known to be skip raiders [laughter] because we're always looking for materials and we usually have limited finances. But for me, using the waste materials was really a conceptual idea as well, taking the waste from the hospital and showing it to people in a different form. It symbolised things that were overlooked or let slide.

SUSAN: I see analogies here to service users, who may be seen as being stuck in hospital and forgotten, and perhaps to the hospital as a place where they are changed and helped. They might not be the same as they were before, but at least they experience something valuable – that would be an ideal way of seeing the relationship between service users and services.

Art and usefulness

KATE: When I work in this environment I feel a responsibility to make something useful. And Albert feels this too. He wants to share the transformation in his own life with other people, so the theme of transformation ran through the whole project.

SUSAN: It's interesting that you as artists who see the beauty in things, you actually almost get infected by the hospital that says 'USEFUL!'. Nurses and clinicians tend to be quite practical. We wanted to be useful and that's probably why we chose the jobs we did. You come in as an artist with a much wider concept and then become infected by the hospital which says well, you know, art's fine, but it's got to be useful art!

ANNE: That accusation is thrown at artists a lot: that they're surplus to requirements or that art's a luxury area to be working in. On the question of usefulness, I want to address what it is the hospital wants. I feel maybe some of the projects have been just a bit too 'out there' in terms of not bringing people on board with them.

SUE: Isn't that a natural way of learning? You have to take risks – some ideas will work, some won't. And the fact that some don't isn't a failure.

SUSAN: I don't know how you decide what kind of projects to do and who you're going to work with. I can see that some of the one-to-one work is hugely rewarding. The ARoundhead project[4] tries to get more people involved. It's a nice idea but I'm not sure what will come out of it. We had a period in May where we got these funny phone calls that made us laugh...

SUE: Isn't that enough? I was having a crap day when you did the pilot, my computer had broken down and I wasn't in a good mood. Then suddenly I got these mad phone calls ... To listen to this man, in dulcet tones, talking nonsense, reciting a little ditty, or asking me silly questions, made me laugh out loud! For me that was the purpose of it.

SUSAN: Maybe it's my own preconceptions, but I feel that there needs to be something more concrete...

KATE: That's really interesting, because there is a balance to be struck between an experience and something material to keep.

SUE: Sometimes I really wonder – and I'm describing me and other non-artists as laypeople in this context – whether artists really understand how foreign their language can be to laypeople. When the ARoundhead concept came up Shona, one of the support workers at the Hearing Voices group[5], handed me a couple of typed sheets and asked if I knew anything about it. I couldn't understand it at all. Shona was doubtful about getting involved because she didn't know what it was about or what the expectations of her would be. Once Caz[6] met her and explained it she was interested, and in fact she brought one of the voice hearers, Steve, over to the workshop and it worked out well.

KATE: I agree with you that the best way of communicating is face to face. It's when people see the person behind the project that they actually engage.

Relationships and expectations

SUSAN: That brings us to the question of relationships and expectations. You're based here and have built up relationships

SUSAN

KATE

ANNE

SUE

within the hospital. But my particular experience with one of the projects was less useful. Although there were a number of meetings with the artist concerned, expectations were never met. Artists coming to work here need to anticipate people's expectations and explain the project fully. That didn't happen – partly to do with the individual artist concerned, and partly to do with the people who became involved as well.

When artists come in for one-off projects we don't really know what their motives are. I don't want to use the term 'vetting', but together we need to do a bit more exploration with people because they're working unsupervised with very vulnerable people. I like art in the hospital but it was a difficult experience and one we need to learn from.

SUE: Induction's too formal a word, but we need to have something like that, perhaps informal meetings with those artists who are new to mental health institutions.

SUSAN: I don't think it does the patients any harm to be challenged provided you are careful and know when to draw back. But from a staff perspective one thing is important: whether you agree with what goes on in psychiatric care, the relationship between the patient and doctor or keyworker at its best is working towards a common goal. Whether that includes medication or any other kind of treatment, it may have taken a lot of negotiation to get to that point. It's fine to hold whatever beliefs you have and even to talk about them if you've gauged the group right. What is unacceptable is to use your own views to potentially undermine that relationship.

KATE: I think the hospital community also need to understand their own prejudices when they come into a situation. Maybe some kind of informal support or training would be helpful for both parties.

Preparing artists and selecting projects

ANNE: This brings us to how we prepare our artists and select the projects. We did try to involve staff in that process last year, but only after the artists had already researched their ideas and worked out who would be involved in their projects. I think in future staff and patients should be involved in selecting the artists and influencing the ideas as much as possible.

SUSAN: I don't believe that the hospital should have a veto on projects because I think one of the most positive aspects of your role is to challenge. We need not be afraid of that, but there has to be some degree of safety for us until we're sure what to expect from a project. That should be made explicit.

SUSAN: How did Steve Duval's project[7] come about, for example? Did he come to you with the idea?

KATE: Well, because Functionsuite was a two-year lottery project, we wanted to bring in artists in a way that allowed some flexibility both for the artists and for the hospital community. We devised a research period to give artists opportunities to meet people and develop ideas.

SUSAN: So the artist would come in and have a look around, discuss ideas, and then come up with a proposal for a particular project?

KATE: Yes. The idea was that the research period would give the artists time to discover things, as we had done ourselves.

ANNE: The remit of our projects is to form collaborations, and I tend to leave things as open as possible, so when we meet there's a kind of open space for something to form out of.

SUE: Rather than you walking in with preconceived ideas, you want to see what the group's going to do?

ANNE: Yes.

SUSAN: In a way that's fine, the project can develop, as you say. But in most of the art projects people are actually involved in creating something. Maybe I'm being too simplistic, but in an Artlink group I expect to have some sort of physical, hands-on creativity.

Matching an artist with a patient

ANNE: The way that Michelle Naismith[8] was brought in to work with Jeanette was quite different. I matched Michelle up to work with Jeanette. Having worked with Jeanette myself I became interested in two artists collaborating with the same person and how different the outcomes might be.

SUSAN: I am curious about why you chose Jeanette. And why would she get an artist or even two artists to herself? How did you come to work with Jeanette in the first place? Did she knock on your door? Did you seek her out?

KATE: I met Jeanette about eight years ago.

ANNE: Did she make any work at that time?

KATE: I'm not sure. I was putting out information about open workshops and she came along, and she's been coming ever since. Over the last six years Jeanette's acknowledgement of herself as an artist has grown.

SUSAN: I think that brings up an important point: if your funding stopped tomorrow how would you disengage? And what happens if somebody says 'Well, actually there's Mary in ward such and such, can you give the resources to her?' How would you deal with that?

ANNE: Well, that's interesting, particularly as Kate's leaving. Jeanette has had the longest working relationship of anybody with us and I am very aware of preparing for that day. It's more likely Jeanette's going to leave us rather than the other way round. Most people move on from here into the community, but there is a gap when people leave, as our remit is to work within the hospitals.

SUSAN: Is there anything you can pass them on to?

ANNE: The main thing we can do is identify opportunities for people when they do move on. It has to be done on an individual basis.

Getting wider involvement

SUE: It would be nice to end this discussion with some brain-storming on how we can help other staff in the hospital to understand your work and how it enriches the inner lives of our service users. If it hadn't been for you, we would have no idea of the creativity inside folk and therefore would never have given them a vehicle to explore it. Think of Jeanette: without this, her life would have been totally different. How can we have your work more widely known and understood?

SUSAN: This comes back to the importance of networking and building up relationships.

SUE: I know, but you can't spread yourself so thin you've no time for the art work itself. I think we have some responsibility for getting staff involved.

SUSAN: People need to understand what's being asked of them and what sort of things that you can offer them. Giving concrete examples of work that you've done, showing its variety, is very helpful.

ANNE: Sometimes I feel that: 'Are we taking more than we're giving?' is a real issue for artists practising in hospital. How much are you giving back, how much are you taking?

SUSAN: It may feel as though you're getting ideas, you're getting inspirations – but patients are getting a lot out of it as well otherwise they wouldn't be involved.

SUE: But we often don't acknowledge that. We assume people know we value their work, but sometimes we need to say it.

SUSAN: I always have the concern that reaching the biggest number of people is the most important thing. But the other side is somebody like Jeanette. The difference in her life is probably more profound than it would be if you'd given forty people an afternoon's pleasure. You can't weigh up these things.

ANNE: About the issue of the small numbers of people that we work with, publishing the book will enable us to share our practice and ideas of collaboration more widely. I know that people are already looking at our work as a model either to copy or to adapt in some way.

SUE: I have really, really enjoyed this discussion.

SUSAN: It's been very useful to have this opportunity. It allows you to look at things from different angles and sparks off other ideas as you go along. Now we can lay the foundations for things to improve, and hopefully get a wider involvement in our work. ■

The Crime of Uglyfication

A play by Jeanette Bell & Michelle Naismith

The Queen: [Shouts.] Oyez, oyez, oyez! Case against the hospital for uglyfying patients and not teaching them crafts and art.

The Prosecutor: [Shouts.] All rise in the name of our people. The Prosecution Counsel wishes to bring up the subject of the uglyfication of patients in mental hospitals and put forward, instead, character building and others' needs for crafts and art.

The Queen: Uglied... The crime of being locked up and uglied in this day and age instead of natural beauty; uglyfication and derision. [A pause.] Case for the Prosecution:

The Prosecutor: Do we want Character and Craftsmanship or do we want death and despair?

The Queen: The evidence is as follows... [She holds up each piece of evidence individually.] Two tiles, handmade with marbles. [She shows them firstly to the King Poodle and then to camera.] Woollen patchwork blankets and/or capes. [She shows her own cape firstly to the King Poodle and then to the audience/camera.] Knitted wigwams (works in progress). [She shows them firstly to the King Poodle and then to camera.] Many paintings including this fine example 'Closing Time' by a certain Jeanette Bell [She shows it firstly to the King Poodle and then to camera.]

The Prosecutor: The Prosecutor also proposes a hairdresser on the wards with no baldening of patients.

The Queen: Case for the Defence:

The Defence Lawyer: The Case for the Defence is as follows: I defend the hospital's policies, there appears to be no hard evidence of a general uglyfication process at play. If there are indeed ugly patients and/or ugly wards, I would suggest this comes more from certain patients' lack of self discipline, coupled with a refusal to comprehend the daily reality of staff shortages, which will inevitably result in a shortage of readily available hands for the daily brushing of medium to long hair.

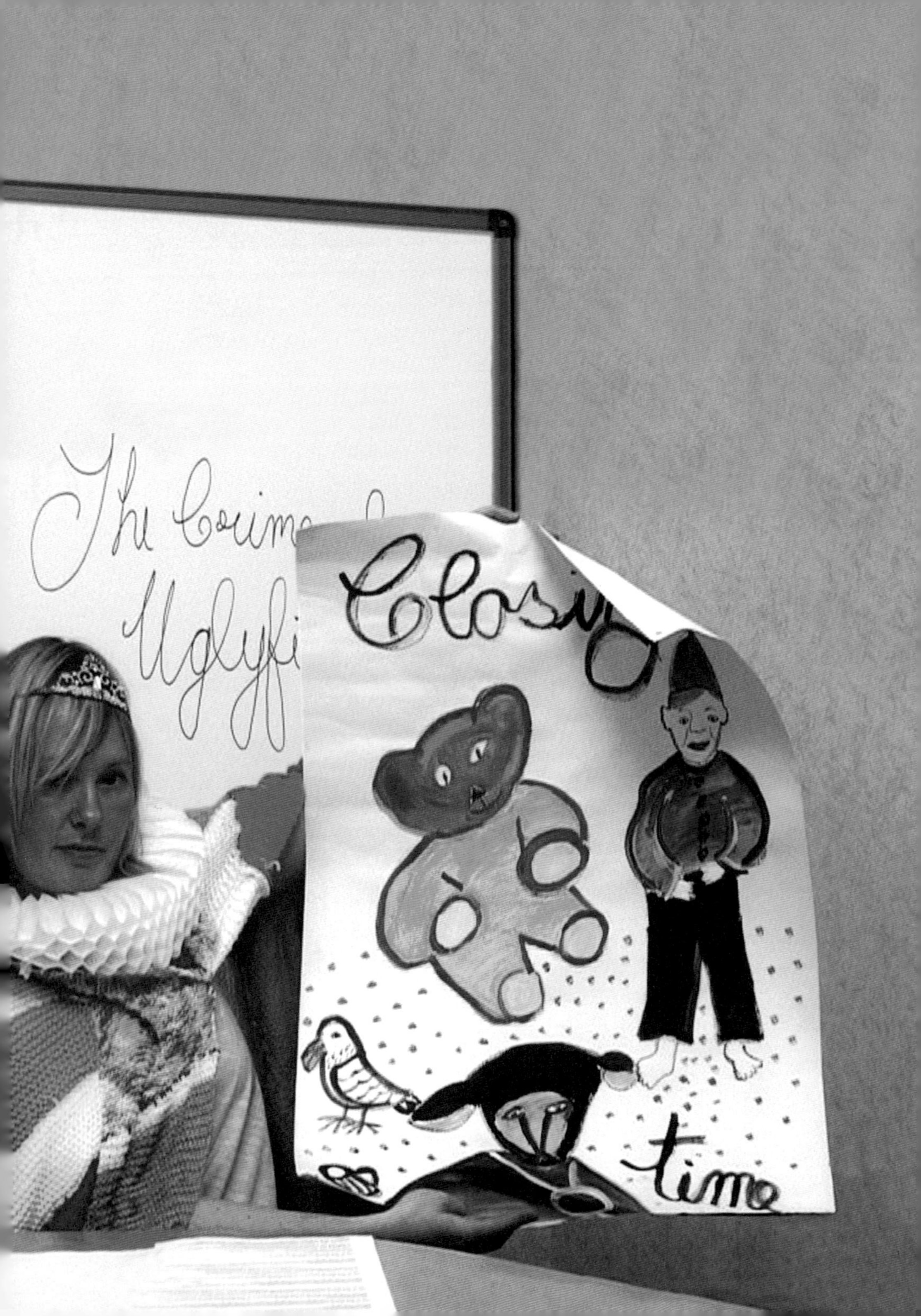
time

In terms of uglyfication of the fabric of the hospital building itself, I would say to you that the uglyfying process is caused mainly by the profusion of graffiti in the corridors.

The Queen: Case for the Prosecution:

The Prosecutor: The writing on the hospital and grounds is a free and readily available means of self-expressionism. You show me examples of graffiti and I'll show you examples of craftsmanship.

The Queen: Case for the Defence:

The Defence Lawyer: Patients eat the wrong food, drink the wrong drinks and chain-smoke like no tomorrow.

The Queen: Case for the Prosecution:

The Prosecutor: The cooked chicken is rubbish.

The Queen: Case for the Defence:

The Defence Lawyer: The abundance of hospital leisure pursuits from the 'Take You Out of Yourself' school of thought remain under-utilised through no faults other than those of self-inflicted introversion and all round shoe-gazing.

The Queen: The case for the Prosecution continues:

The Prosecutor: It is difficult for people to self-motivate if they feel they have been 'uglyfied' or have had their character reduced. There is ill-informed decoration and design everywhere: corridors, wards, offices, staff canteens... We would suggest it takes more than extensive use of 'good for nothingness' wood-look trellis and 'a hint of' nothing-in-particular pastel shades from the cheapskate paint warehouse to create a harmonious ambience. Patients driven to animal senses need to swipe back.

The Queen: As further evidence both for Prosecution and Defence, some examples of graffiti from the hospital: on an outside bench – 'The Persecutors Will Become The Persecuted'. On a toilet roll holder in the 'ladies' – 'The Power Sucks'. Graffiti by Jeanette Bell – 'Remember Your Worth'; 'Stop Intimidation'; 'A Thing Of Beauty Is A Joy Forever'; 'All That Glitters Is Not Gold'; 'No Wicked End – The Cat Has Got The Cream Off Me'; 'May All Your Joys Be Little Ones'. A hospital porter writes: 'Knowledge is Treacherous'. Voilà! [A pause.]

The Queen: The King Poodle will now consider the verdict. [A pause.]

The King Poodle has reached a verdict and will have the last word on this unfortunate matter: I speak on behalf of the King... There will be no more uglyfication in hospitals. There will be from this day forth character building, Crafts and Art. An award-winning hairdresser from Glasgow will be appointed to the hospital. Graffiti will now be referred to as hand-written, public signage and viewed as a valid means of self-expression. The fabric of the hospital building will be, from this moment on, public property.

The Prosecutor: The King Poodle has spoken. [Shouts.] No more crimes of uglyfication.

END

Lines of Resistance to Human Misery[1]

John Beagles

Feeling bored, and finding myself increasingly mute and powerless within the institutional authority of art school, I was attracted at the age of twenty to the work of artist Jo Spence. Her analysis of the impact her background had had on her adult identity, in terms of feelings of anger, class shame and invisibility, had a profound impact on me.

Spence built her 'anti-art career' out of a painfully honest unravelling of the riddle of herself. She believed in the transformative power of dialogue and the therapeutic value of personal storytelling. Like the other artists mentioned in this essay, Spence was passionate about the power of art and language to develop what Italo Calvino called 'lines of resistance to human misery'. A therapist, community art worker, writer and lecturer as well as an artist, she worked wholeheartedly with others: for example in the 1970s she was involved in the Photographic Workshop, a collaborative, community-based project.

In her essays and photo works, Spence sought to 'control' the impact her past continued to exert on her present. This was achieved through an unflinching, almost forensic examination of 'herstory'. Working in collaboration, most notably with Rosy Martin, she sought to bring back to life the repressed traumas of the past in what she referred to as phototherapy. In a kind of theatre of the self, Spence playfully took on the role of her mother, her younger self, and her future older self, in order to materialise repressed traumas and face future threatening ones. As with all of her work, the aim was to wrestle back some control over her history, as well as offer viewers the possibility of transforming their own identities through the application of similar strategies. Hers was a perverse, contradictory practice, by turns funny and self-deprecating, theoretical and serious, pragmatic and interventionist. Perversely for the context of this essay, her greatest battle came not with

Project: The Crime of Uglyfication

Jeanette Bell and I began working together by recording all our conversations, many of which included discussions about daily problems and obstacles faced by patients in a psychiatric hospital. Using these conversations as a base, we constructed a fiction that became The Crime of Uglyfication.
– Michelle Naismith, artist

the confidence-sapping ghosts of her past, but with the medical profession. She suffered from breast cancer and later leukaemia (from which she died in 1992), and her experiences as a patient generated painfully raw photographic work that exposed the routine, naturalised dehumanisation of the health service at the time (this was during the 1980s). As such, this work was a plea for patients to be recognised as subjects with personalities as opposed to potential cadavers.

Such a little thing

In Spence's documentary work about her experiences of 1980s health care, she explicitly revealed the manner in which patients were routinely and systematically made invisible and powerless. Michelle Naismith and Jeanette Bell's video, The Crime of Uglyfication, similarly draws attention to the invisible workings of power, to assert that patients are more than simply bodies to be processed. However, while Spence's work was partly infused with a realist documentary feel, Naismith and Bell's work is a twisted trial, which presents a case against the hospital 'for uglyfying patients and not teaching them crafts and art'.

In the mock trial (or should that be mock turtle, for there's more than a hint of Alice in Wonderland) the pleas for the defence and prosecution are presided over by a hybrid entity. On the other side of the looking glass, the curly weave of the high court judge's wig has been replaced by the coiffured perm of a poodle costume.

A script for a short courtroom drama that was videoed and then premiered at the Cameo cinema, Edinburgh, in March 2005.

The matter-of-fact naturalness in which the scene is portrayed, as well as the blind indifference of the protagonists to the dog/human presence, allude to the potential absurdity of artists working within hospitals.

In the debate, counsel for and against bat around the conflicts at the heart of patient care. These might be thought to be irresolvable, but of course they're not – it's just that the political will to resolve them resides beyond the confines of the hospital and the art world. In defending the hospital against the charge of reducing people's character, of eroding their sense of self (the very invisibility Spence sought to resist), the defence justly responds that such criticisms reveal 'a refusal to comprehend the daily reality of staff shortages'. The defence might have added how present-day hospital failings are the consequence of successive, shortsighted decisions – from the construction of atrocious concrete slab buildings to general cuts and on to the looming disaster of PFI.[2] Whether they like it or not, artists must face up to the fact that, within this culture and against this backdrop, art is often nothing more than an occasionally soothing balm.

The artist Terry Atkinson once said that all artists should be working to work themselves out of a job, the implication being that if art could truly transform society, then there would, come the day of universal happiness etc., be no need for art. Unfortunately for us, we are unlikely to witness this new age dawning, so in the meantime little things and little gestures, meagre as they

The waiting room, Accident & Emergency,
Royal Infirmary of Edinburgh

might seem, are all we have to cling to. Naismith and Bell's video mentions the introduction of a hairdresser at the hospital, or the possibility of daily visits to an art gallery, and these may seem trivial details. But they are vital reminders of the need to retain a commitment to activities that are not governed by waiting lists or targets. It is art and craft's 'uselessness' in a culture increasingly enslaved to narrow economic ideas of value that makes it so appealing and potentially restorative. In this sense, too, Naismith and Bell's absurd, 'useless' video is the perfect tonic.

No time for talking

For her project, Ilana Halperin was hoping to reveal the various ways members of the accident & emergency department manage to work in a zone of continual crisis. Motivated in part by her own recent experiences of medical care, she had aimed to give a voice to the traditionally stoic, professional carer, whose full-time job it is to listen and empathise. Collaborating with Dennis Purcell, one of the nurses at the hospital, Halperin had aimed to highlight how the tales of the emergency room staff are potentially a rich, compelling source of narrative, the latent possibilities of which are all the more enticing because they are routinely ignored or passed over. In this respect, her project connects with Jo Spence's interests in the political and therapeutic power of storytelling, specifically the narration of stories that usually remain untold.

>>

Stories from the A+E

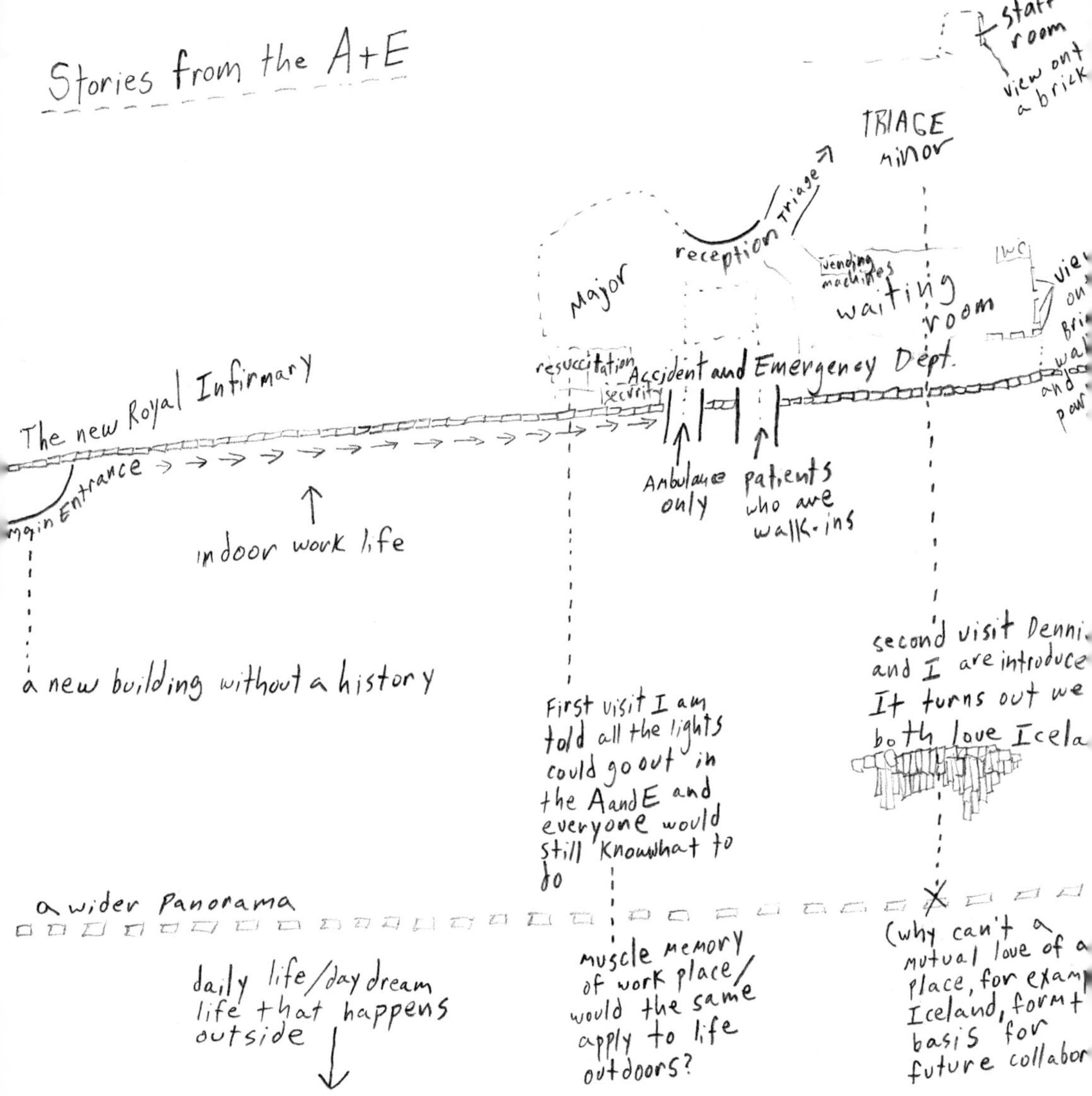

staff room
view out
a brick

TRIAGE
minor

reception / triage

Major

vending machines

waiting room

IWC

view on Bri

wal and pow

The new Royal Infirmary

resuccitation

security

Accident and Emergency Dept.

main Entrance →→→→

↑
indoor work life

Ambulance only

patients who are walk-ins

a new building without a history

second visit Denni and I are introduce It turns out we both love Icela

First visit I am told all the lights could go out in the A and E and everyone would still know what to do

a wider Panorama

daily life/day dream
life that happens
outside
↓

muscle memory of work place/ would the same apply to life outdoors?

(why can't a mutual love of a place, for exam Iceland, form t basis for future collabor

Key: ▭▭▭ = in and around the hospital
▭▭▭▭ = the world outside
┊ = how one thing leads to another
∕∕ = where things led nowhere
▦ = where things happened
X = transition points

new panoramas for
the waiting room
to open up the view.
Strata studies to read
while you wait.

craigmillar Castle behind the hospital

--roger the
seismologist

Deliver talk
based on
'strata stories! Moments before
2 recussitation calls
are put out on the
loudspeaker.
Few staff are
able to attend
a result.

we plan a lunch for
staff on the castle
grounds. No one can
come.

invited too.

ta study,
es from inside
utside the A&E
reams, hanggliding,
op of Arthur's Seat,
faraway beaches
ound in conversation.

I receive
an invitation
to help
redesign the
waiting room.

artists talk in
one room of
the A&E.
Emergency in the
other.

a path leads
up a hill
connecting
the hospital
grounds to
a wider panorama
with a long
history.

geological risk/
working in a
high risk situation
stress

second talk
cancelled due
to staff shortages.

Meet with staff
select the color of new grass for the waiting room X

Art can fulfil its age-old purpose of decorating and enhancing, as a kind of icing on the architect's cake. Or it can confront the institution – in this case the Accident and Emergency department – and ask questions and make something out of the result, an approach that is less about the building and more about the whole world of A&E. It's a bit risky. The outcome is unforeseen at the start, or it will be if anything interesting is to happen.

The Functionsuite project in A&E started in that open ended way. It ended by making a partial transition to the decorative approach, but I think something interesting was carried over from the original path.

I work in A&E. I am a nurse practitioner. At one time, I was an art student. There had been some talk in A&E about decorating our new waiting room. There was an assumption around that the word 'artist' was just a shorter way of saying 'waiting room muralist'. I knew as soon as I saw Ilana that 'waiting room muralist' was wide of the mark. Her manner and style was hushed, receptive, soft, as if a major part of her work was to listen to people.

The whole thing went along for about a year and a half, in little bursts with long gaps. The theme which I saw emerging for the project was integration: how staff in A&E use the capacities that they develop in their work when they are outside, and how the department fits into the social and geological environment.

Ilana ran into some solid obstacles. A&E staff were asked to involve themselves by contributing stories and joining in little expeditions to explore the area around the hospital. A&E is multilayered in a curious way. To a casual eye it can seem chaotic. It is subdivided into little operational villages, so that its massive flow of activity, fifteen hundred patients a week pouring through the doors, can be managed. We are pressured during every working minute, and we cannot feel comfortable when we step away from the coalface, even for activities which are designed to improve our work, such as training. Ilana might have been able to engage the staff in telling their stories and exploring their environment, but only if she had been able to camp in the department and make it happen.

Ilana did what she had to do. She backed off, reconsidered and came back from a different angle. And now we have some images in our waiting room.

The thing that she has carried over from the first attempt is the idea of integration, that the people inside the place also live in the outer world, and that the little hothouse bubble of the department is part of a larger thing. And for us, who work in there, and for those patients and their relatives too, whose time there can be vivid, harsh and painful or drearily interminable, they give just a glimpse of a larger world.

– Dennis Purcell

A story from a nurse practitioner in the A&E

The weather is so mercurial. One of the oddities about the weather in Iceland is that if you pass through the same place on different days, depending on the sky, the place seems to have a longer horizon than Scotland. In Scotland you are always meeting your mountain. Iceland actually has a feeling; it's like a very large plain. It does have mountains but they are on the fringe. You see this very big sky and the way the sky looks determines the landscape. On different days seeing the same landscape is not like being in the same place because actually the nature of the sky changes the experience completely.

A story from a senior house officer in the A&E

Arthur's Seat is my favourite place to go and relax. I like the roughness of the rocks. I also like the softness of the flowers and the green of the trees. I really like the rocks because they are brown but they are topped with black. They kind of look like they have been burned so they're very active. I was there yesterday. It's beautiful now, blossoming with yellow bushes and the grass in front of Arthur's Seat is so nice and bright and smooth. I like the differences, the contrasts, and I like the colour.

>> Just as Naismith and Bell sought to make visible the invisible workings of power within the hospital, so Halperin, by listening to the professional listener and carer, hoped to make audible the unheard voices of the staff. Institutionally, doctors and nurses may possess authority and power, but personally they are as vulnerable and potentially as isolated as the patients. In working with members of the hospital such as Dennis Purcell, Halperin was attempting to create a far more complex, self-produced representation of nurses and doctors, one that countered the comforting myth of angels and heroes.

However, as with many projects dependent upon the collaborative input of others, real life rudely disrupted Halperin's plans. A salutary reminder, perhaps, that self-reflection and relaxed conversation are unattainable luxuries for the overworked and underpaid, the pressures of working in the hospital decisively altered the nature of her project. Minutes before her first talk, an ER emergency pulled all the attending staff away, while subsequent attempts to restart the project were again compromised by staff shortages and heavy workloads. Faced with the realisation that the pragmatic demands of hospital work were wholly incompatible with her own perhaps over-idealised aims, Halperin had to radically rethink what she could actually accomplish.

The hospital offered what on the surface appeared to be an unattractive alternative route for her – they required their waiting room to be redesigned. On the face of it, such a practical task didn't seem too enticing; however, Halperin had always intended to be adaptable, 'seeing where the process took her'. Fairly quickly, Halperin realised that, contrary to her perhaps rather formal attempts to initiate dialogue, working in that space offered the opportunity to stay true to her initial interest in teasing out narratives from staff, but in a far more natural manner. As she said, 'It became clear that the only way I could talk to staff in more depth was to spend a lot of time hanging out in their staff room talking to them on the sly.'

Project: A Knitting Bee

The work I do with patients has little effect on the institution as a whole, but it does have a great effect on the individuals involved.
– Anne Elliot, core Functionsuite artist

Collaborate Fully

An important aspect of many of the artists' Functionsuite projects is a determination to ensure that the artists build up genuine, long-term relationships with the patients and staff. The friendships and collaborations that Jeanette Bell (who has resided at the Royal Edinburgh Hospital for eight years) has had with Kate Gray, and more recently Anne Elliot and Michelle Naismith, are exemplary.

All of the cooperative work with Bell[3] has been founded upon a shared desire to help each other challenge and break their patterns of thought. In Bell's work with Elliot, they explored the possibility of using art to disrupt the feelings of dependency and boredom that inevitably arise from long-term residency within an institution.

For Elliot, her conversations with Bell have resulted in a frank reappraisal of what it means to cooperate with someone else, and more centrally to rethink the value and meaning of art. The foundation of their collaboration is non-hierarchical, a conversation between equals; as Bell remarks, 'I was cooperating with her. It was joint thought.' Central to this cooperative work has been an understanding of, and a belief in, the potentially transformative and redeeming power of conversation. As Bell says, 'I am used to giving warnings about how I have had failures in my life and how they couldn't have been avoided.'

>>

the Link Gallery

Jeanette Bell and Anne Elliot invited knitters Margaret McIntyre and Margaret Watson to join them in creating a blanket. Amidst the knitting, Jeanette would constantly draw. These drawings become the catalyst for photographs that Anne took, which were attempts to make these drawings real.

>> This genuine, long-term commitment to investing time in the relationship may on the surface appear straightforward, but unfortunately many community or public art projects have been compromised precisely because of an absence of dedicated time. Part of the problem is that there is a powerful demand to see quantifiable, easily documented, physical evidence of 'art in the community', with a particular emphasis on projects that satisfy administrative criteria and tick appropriate political boxes. Time and friendship aren't quantifiable in these terms; it is perhaps precisely because of this that they are so valuable.

So, while many initiatives are built around the creation of recognisable art objects, Functionsuite has focused on the need to create social networks involving the artists, the hospitals and Functionsuite as an organisation. Anne Elliot in particular places great emphasis on this. While the creation of photographs, videos or temporary sculptures is an important aspect of her work, she regards the communal, collaborative process of producing the work as an equally creative act in and of itself. Elliot's practice as an artist involves being a catalyst for a creativity that bridges divides between patients and carers, and artists and patients. The recent Knitting Bee project, where patients and staff alike were invited to participate, is a good example of this. Here, the social, collaborative aspects of art production were as important as the end result.

Confronting your own powerlessness, especially when sick, is a disturbing affair. In such situations, perhaps the last thing you

This gave Jeanette some of her self-esteem back and it showed she has got a lot to give. It gave her a goal. Before this, there was nothing to stimulate her.
– Margaret Dickson, cousin of Jeanette Bell

need is someone offering fantastical promises of hope and restoration. As a twenty-year-old, I found Jo Spence instructive because she always tempered her passion for art with a healthy dose of realism – there were never any promises that art was a miracle cure. Today, when art gets involved with the public, the art world often gets rather over-excited about its mission, its power, and its impact. Fortunately, Functionsuite shares Spence's healthy mix of optimism and realism – like Spence it refuses to trade in false hopes and magical cures, acknowledging instead the importance of dialogue, collaboration and contact. ■

The 'C' Word
Alison Stirling

An artist says, *'There is no such thing as arts collaboration. It doesn't work.'*

I respond, *'Forget about the word: it's about working together.'*

The artist leans back, folds his arms and repeats, *'There is no such thing as arts collaboration.'*

Today, many artists are interested in the idea of collaboration, but for many, the emphasis remains on being identified as the main facilitator/director of the collaborative artwork, either as gallery artist or as artist working within communities – in effect, replicating a gallery practice in a public domain. It appears that the word itself – collaboration – has become overused to the point where it loses its meaning and potential, and so linked to disappointment, so not-what-we-wanted-it-to-be, that to use it feels almost like swearing. I remember going to a talk about the Royston Road Project,[1] a respected community arts initiative in Glasgow. I kept thinking 'but it can't all be as rosy as everyone's saying it is. What hasn't worked? Have the artists really reflected the interests of the residents and, if so, how come the artwork that they make individually to show in galleries looks exactly the same?'

In this age of the split community, in which we are fearful of the person we sit next to, never mind our neighbours or colleagues, the idea of working together seems very necessary. It is important that we promote some notion of community both at home and at work. Within the arts, this means we need to open out our artistic approaches and create the time and space to learn from other people. Then, if we can resist the temptation to pretend that everything is working well, and pay attention to what's not working as well as what is, we can perhaps begin to create something relevant.

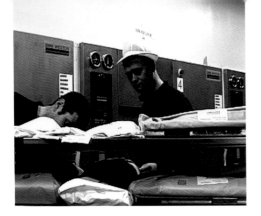

Project: The Comic Project

This project had a direct effect on the morale of the department as a whole because Gordon was making drawings about his work environment and his relationships with his co-workers. He showed in a humorous way what the department does from a worker's point of view. His drawings are everywhere in the department and they lift the spirits of the place.

– Garry Gorham, Gordon Dickson's line manager

Finding Ways to Work Together

I am on top of a scaffold with my friend, the artist Brian Jenkins. We are part of an artists' programme, working with people with learning disabilities, each of whom is representing a European country. We are to make twelve 6-metre-high paintings to be exhibited in Luxembourg City as part of its year as Cultural Capital of Europe. We are having trouble with Greece. Italy's painting isn't looking too good either, and the care worker for the Greek participant, who fancies herself as an artist, has opinions about how the painting should be finished. Italy stands quietly awaiting instruction and we all start arguing. It goes on for quite a while. *'Excuse me.'* We continue to argue. *'EXCUSE ME.'* We look down at Germany. *'Do you not think you should ask Italy what she wants to do? After all, it is her painting.'*

Within the Functionsuite project, everyone was a collaborator, willing or otherwise, whether administrator, doctor, nurse, porter, telephonist, patient, artist, director of Artlink, anthropologist, project manager, or publication editor. Devising ways for these disparate people to work together did not happen overnight and we were dependent on available levels of creativity, humour, imagination, time and flexibility within each sometimes difficult pairing. It also required from all of us the highest levels of patience. Think about it: a cross-section of arts and healthcare people who don't know one another and who have their own definition of art. On top of that, the people from the hospitals

are all busy doing something else – their jobs. And the artists are finding that 'the usefulness of their occupation is immediately questioned and art is forced to confront a raw world'.[2]

Not Knowing

It is the detail that interests me, the small, accumulated experiences informing our actions, of how the situation is established and how we build our understanding of each other. It is amongst that detail, in the crossovers between people, that the real collaboration lies. I'm interested in what's there and how we learn to work with it, positively manipulate it, work with each other and only then turn it into an artwork. The best way to achieve this is to instigate conversations between people and use them as a way of informing what could be. For example, if in conversation we find that a pathologist likes knitting then, if he is interested, we could use that as the starting point of a project. We want to open up the institution, work with people as they are and see where that takes us. We create the space and time to develop ideas in relation to what we discover.

In practice, it can immediately create confusion: confusion for the artist whose practice is questioned, challenged and at points negated; confusion for the hospital, as they do not know what to expect; and confusion for Functionsuite staff who must navigate through this apparent disparity.

The artmaking process is a process of not knowing. It is true that we can ground our knowing in models and best practices, and through new art genres and mechanisms that realize inclusive, collaborative, participatory, remedial, and transformative ways of working ... It is these core aims that allow us to both know (based on our past experience and that of others) and to trust in our not knowing (so that we can reinvent according to new circumstances, and realize each project in its own time and space).
– Mary Jane Jacob [3]

Functionsuite based its work on this model of 'not knowing'. We did start, admittedly, with the knowledge that there was a history of real interest in the arts within the hospitals. We were also familiar with many of the staff and knew that they were willing to experiment.[4] We also knew that a lot of artists would be excited about the possibilities. But what we really didn't know was how projects would turn out.

Ways of Involving

When I was a child, I would walk around the playground shouting 'Who wants a game of ... ?' If another child thought the game worth playing, we would link arms and shout for others to join in. When we had enough players, we'd start our game.

>>

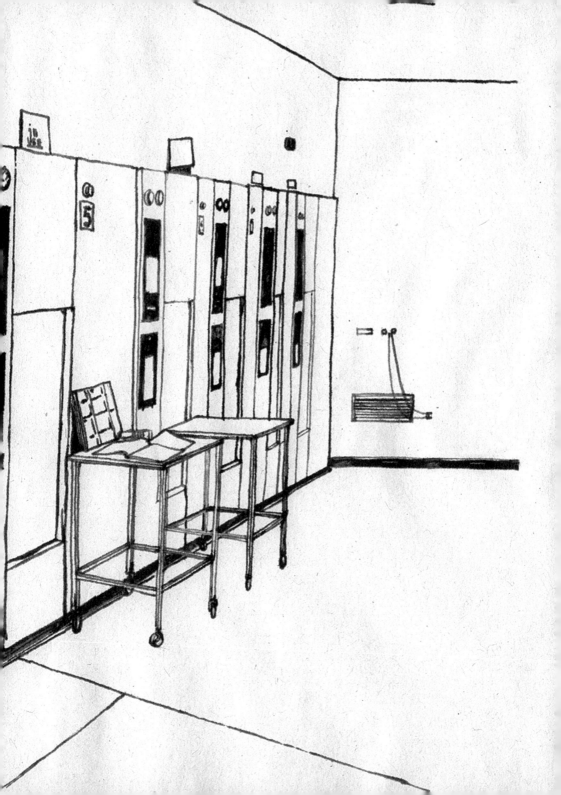

>> I'm now going to discuss three of the Functionsuite projects. In relation to this game: one artist found a friend to play with, but found it so hard to meet up that they ran out of time; one couldn't find the right people to play with and ended up playing on her own; and the other found lots of people to play with but couldn't decided which game to play.

The Comic Project

Mick Peter and Gordon Dickson were matched in what turned out to be an imperfect pairing. Gordon works in the HSDU (sterilising unit) at the Royal Infirmary. He works long shifts and to entertain himself and others he makes caricatures of the people with whom he works. Kate Gray (core Functionsuite artist) stumbled across him whilst making a film about life in the hospital basement. She suggested that artist Mick Peter could work with Gordon to make a comic book.

Mick was keen on a collaboration in which Gordon's input would be equal to his own. However, his collaborator's circumstances made this very difficult. Gordon was too busy; the department he worked in was understaffed. The project drifted along and, having spent most of the time allocated to them just arranging to meet, they finally ran out of time. The reality of working within the hospital, with its totally different set of priorities, challenged the artist's preconceptions of collaboration. Shattered expectations are common, and the success of the project – the fact that they did sometimes manage to meet and make drawings – is down to the artist's persistence in coming back again and again. According to Mick, what they had in common was as much the cups of tea they drank and the conversations they had as the drawing. This project is best viewed as a 'work in progress', a snapshot of the point at which the actual artwork is only just beginning, which is in fact the most difficult part of any project.

Anna Best takes notes whilst touring the laundry facilities at St John's Hospital

Unchain the Lunatics: two stories[1]
by Anna Best

Loss of reason and enthusiasm are the main symptoms of this particular condition. In medical language it is known as Hyperenthusia, treatable by _____.

She is well known historically for recording her visions of men's sexual parts. Given half a chance she will bring up the subject, her love of certain penises. She had absolutely no occupation, entertainment, over a period of 10 years. Her diet and hygiene were both dealt with on an intermittent basis. Food consisted of _____, custard and gravy.

Her friends went to look for a motorised chair that could lower her into a hot bath, and raise her up out of it again. One of them had made the mistake of trying to lift her out of the bath – having to get in the bath, support her under the armpits and heave her upwards – a back breaking and terrifying feat for both of them. Not being able to lift up your own body anymore. That kind of weakness of body – where one wishes only to feed the body on chocolate – as if it's a separate animal lying in a cage across the road ... the shock to find oneself attached to that very body, unable to make it do what you want – is that what it's like? – the body so vast it has become immobile.

In his case, the body is so frail, and reduced to merely bones, that to stand becomes unthinkable, the pins won't straighten – they buckle involuntarily.

They won't support the tiniest of bodies now become all ribcage and shoulder blades – packed into the curvature of a warped spine.

In her case the head continues – revelling in its capacities for thoughts and proposed deeds – relishing the little movements that can occur. Associationist theories, falsely or unreasonably associating ideas, is one of her great strengths.

From the courtyard – 'the patients mainly are, most of them, unable to move and need Zimmer frames, seat belts in wheelchairs, they are deaf, dumb and blind. They don't focus on television or read or talk. They scream and shout and hit each other, very often quite seriously. Many sleep from about 9 pm for 12 hours though some go to bed at 2 am, walking the passages of each unit and opening other people's doors. ... There is nothing to do at all. I think each unit should have a small library with a bible, Shakespeare, a good atlas, encyclopaedia and dictionary, if not more. Also a small room should be given to art, ping-pong and games like scrabble. There should be all sorts of classes for exercises and breathing, ideally a swimming pool and gentle outdoor games in the summer like bowling and basketball.

Boredom severely runs the place from the residents' point of view. ... occasionally there is a little music or quizzes. Essentially nothing to do at all. We are locked in our unit – the only thing good is it's clean. ... If the centre could afford a small bus we could travel on a nice day to local sites, see gardens; go to films and art exhibitions etc. The locked doors prevent us from going outside to the 4 or 5 terraces or gardens, or indeed to other units to meet other people who reside there. At least we could have sunshine, wind, and fresh air. ... We are all treated like lost animals who don't live in the real world...'.[2]

The wind has gone out of his sails. His eyes are melting, as old men's eyes do – watery, diluting into something, the soul dissolving perhaps – his spirits are as low as the whisky glass is full on the hour. This brings a wind of pervasive and persuasive sullen sad melancholy, when he stubbornly will not go outdoors or eat or wash himself. The whole of life, the whole of the world, could not be an inspiration. For he is in possession, possessed by a beast, or monkeys, demons, or the devil, however you want to put it.

The orphan in all of us can be detected by a curious old piece of scientific enquiry known as The Wild Beast Test. This was developed at the very end of the eighteenth century in a southern part of Scotland at an institution by the sea. The waves were sometimes the most colourful part of the scenery in that little port. The thinking behind the test is not recorded and can only be guessed at. Patients were to sit, facing out to sea, every day for one hour in the morning and one in the evening, at dawn and at dusk, watching the waves. Each one would reach a point where they began to spot creatures, or wild beasts, in the waves. The staff would ignore this and after some more time had elapsed the patients would become frantic and it was at this time, when the patient was absolutely certain of their sighting that two items of information would be recorded. One was the nature of the wild beast, and the other was the amount of time the patient had taken to arrive at this mental state. These varying amounts of time were found to be most curiously connected with the varying amounts of parenting the patient had been accustomed to. A great difference was found between those whose parents had doted on them from day one and never left their sides and those who had been thrust into an orphanage or foster home. It is quite easy to imagine which group found the wild beasts sooner.

The writer's note to the reader.

Unchain the Lunatics: two stories reflects my working process – meeting people, writing a proposal without an outcome, taking the train, trying to work collaboratively from a distance in various ways, things dissolving and taking different directions. I visited a general hospital, spent time in the Royal Edinburgh, a psychiatric hospital, and got interested in asylums, partly through going to the Bangour Village Hospital (an old asylum now being developed as private housing) and partly through looking into nursing homes for my mother. I thought a lot about the paradox of care and control, security and confinement. The debates about what collaboration is seem to touch on similar issues of control, freedom and power.

Eventually, I invented a writing system based on a fantastic website I found, which included a Mental Health History Timeline.[3] In writing, clarity or definition in a descriptive or explanatory narrative is a kind of confinement. I wanted my writing to be quite elusive, as if it is a kind of freedom.

I have questioned collaboration, what it can be, how it is becoming defined and almost standardised within the art world, how difficult it really is, how easy it is! I had conversations with Justin Kenrick[4] about this, in which he said that every exchange is potentially a form of collaboration. Personally, I am very aware of the imbalance in authorship in many art collaborations, my own included: i.e. the artist gets a commission and asks someone else to contribute, and the power sharing, in terms of the process and the end product, is not equal. I have often worried about this: I ask myself 'am I collaborating properly?' and 'are the participants getting anything out of it?' But I think this is a rather narrow and literal view of what can be a dynamic process of keeping a situation open for as long as possible. Perhaps having a long conversation is a positive result; perhaps participants saying no and knowing why they are saying it is also a good outcome. I don't have answers, but I feel there is too much need for evidence or results in art collaborations.

Dominic, a patient at the Royal Edinburgh who was introduced to me by Anne Elliot[5], was the only person who wanted to have a correspondence with me.[6] He writes beautiful poetry and graffiti on the walls not only of the hospital, but also along the streets that surround it, and in the local supermarket. While I was visiting, the staff tried to persuade him to only write in certain places! The idea of confining graffiti is like confining thought. Dominic and I wrote to each other a bit, but it was rather mundane and mostly about my babies, on their way or when they had arrived, and the weather. Again I was thwarted!

In Unchain the Lunatics: two stories I have included bits of this writing, and I also used the material which I carried away in my head after the many conversations and encounters I had with a whole array of people, including those who are officially part of the context, such as patients or doctors, and others with whom I had an incidental chat on the phone. Accessing what was in my own head, and approaching the idea of context in a conceptual rather than a physical way, I experienced a sense of great freedom. Particularly because of the distance I was working from, all my ideas on how to collaborate, such as setting up an email writing group, were great as ideas. But they never got off the ground, they somehow dissolved, people said 'no', or never responded, or felt they couldn't be frank enough while still working for the hospitals. This was the way the project went and I didn't want to force the situation, respecting the fact that people say no to artists' proposals and incorporating that refusal into how I worked.

Anna Best with Bill Wallace in a tour of the laundry facilities at St John's Hospital.

>> Unchain the Lunatics: two stories

Artist Anna Best had so many ideas, derived from personal experiences. There were so many things she wanted to do, and she would write and write and write. She wanted to explore issues that were important to her, such as anonymity, authorship, asylum, confinement and care, and the struggle to find sense in things. She toured hospital departments and met groups, and she tried different approaches. After a time, her personal circumstances meant that it became impossible for her to come and visit the hospitals.[5] From a distance, she tried email links with writers' groups as well as telephoning and writing to possible collaborators, but she really began her project when she discovered the 'Mental Health History Timeline' by Andrew Roberts.[6] She used phrases extracted from it to spark her own writing.

What Anna could actually achieve evolved in relation to her situation. As a result, the project became inconclusive in certain ways. She did not form a relationship with any one person within the hospital, and perhaps her own ideas were so particular that it made it harder for other people to find a way in. For Anna, collaboration turned out to be a process of establishing the Functionsuite team as a support network and gleaning a certain amount of information from hospital staff and patients.

Project: ...and the trainees

Monthly luncheons with invited guests from the artistic and hospital communities. The meals created time and space in which to share personal and professional experiences and discuss artistic, social and political ideas.

In the two previous projects, there was an underlying sense of urgency for the artists, born out of a need to realise their projects, to evidence the collaboration, to work within very tight time limits. '...and the trainees' perhaps illustrates a more relaxed approach, a way of working which allows the time and space to relax and watch, listen and learn. Artist Anne Elliot's intention was simple: no pressure, no need to make things, no need to hurry. For this project she chose to meet with people, make them lunch, chat and get to know them, before starting to talk about how to make real any ideas. She began by meeting with Sue Robertson, a clinical development nurse who trains healthcare staff on self-harm and suicide. Over lunch they would ask one another questions, first about the possible art projects on which they could collaborate and later about art, healthcare, mental health, travel, food, asylum and Sue's interest in Cher's music and style. Anne showed Sue her artwork and in turn attended Sue's training workshops on self-harm. Sometimes they would invite other people from Functionsuite or the hospital to take part in their discussions. By watching training videos and art films, for example, they would look at the crossover in their activities, and return to the idea of possibly doing an art project together. Artistic ideas are just beginning, and whatever results from this approach will be built upon a solid foundation of mutual understanding and respect. This project is about the fact that it takes time to establish a strong relationship and without that relationship, collaboration can only be superficial.

>>

What is your favourite artwork? (and why)

Who is your favourite artist?

Do you think art made within the hospital context should be functional?

What do you think about artists like Tracey Emin (bed) and Damien Hirst (chopped up cow). After dinner!

>> Building Trust

What has been established is a foundation of trust, involving hospital departments in a variety of projects, gaining participation where we feared there might be none. This was achieved through a delicate balance of trying, failing and at other times succeeding. We took risks in how people were involved, in how the artist established relationships with their collaborators and in expecting the unexpected.

Functionsuite highlighted flaws in the ways in which socially engaged programmes are often established, pointing to possible 'next stage' solutions which respond more deeply to the complexities of collaboration. After all, how can we expect to place artists within diverse communities and ask them to make relevant artworks without first ensuring that they have the time and support to understand that context? It doesn't happen with ease anywhere else, so why should it happen in the arts? What is needed is the development of support networks around artist and collaborator, ensuring that their involvement is grounded in mutual understanding. By this I mean we support artists to apply a 'watch and learn approach' as a starting point to their work with people, ensuring that whatever they make reflects the interests of the people they make it with or for.

For Artlink, this way of working will enable us to listen to the hospital community, and value what they know and bring to the

process, shaping the work as well as its meaning and informing its outcome.[7] If we can build on what we have learned, then the risk is no longer in how people are involved but in how far the flexibility of artistic interpretation can go.

I think we might be getting somewhere. Give it time.

12 November 2003, 11–12 am. Excerpt from diary:

I have just had my first conversation with a member of staff in relation to my new project: looking at their interests and developing artworks around them ... I chose Sue Robertson because she has been involved with hospital arts before and she is very open about her interests outside work.

18 February 2004

Dear Sue,
How are you? I have been thinking about our meetings.
I love the informal arrangement we have. This is a new
kind of relationship for me within the hospital. Since
our last lunch together I have been thinking about staff
break times and how people use them. Could we explore
issues of time through this project? ...

Also, would you like to see some examples of my artwork
over lunch? ...

Anne

From Sue Robertson
Date: Wed, Feb 18, 2004, 1:10 pm
Subject: Time...

Hi Anne
What a delightful letter you sent me! I agree we have a
great relationship for an institutional setting! ...
Time sounds like an intriguing topic ...

Cheers Sue

Lunch 25 February 2004 1 pm
Caz, Anna Best[1], Kate, Charlotte, Sue and Anne
Paneer cheese and spinach with rice.

Sue described us (as artists) as thinking differently from the way she did as a healthcare professional. She spoke about music, types of psychiatrists and psychologists, approaches to male/female treatment and therapy/clothing/hair preferences – basically what makes us different.
– Charlotte Collingwood

8 March 2004. Excerpt from diary:

Sue offered all the artists involved in the Functionsuite project the chance to attend awareness training in self-harm and suicide, alcoholism, manic depression etc. This got me thinking about the idea of 'training' ... Is what Sue and I are doing training each other?

Date: Tues Mar 23 2004 2.51 pm
Subject: re: lunch and planning meeting

Hi Sue
Are you coming for lunch at 12.30pm on Wednesday?
I enjoyed the conversation last week I hope it didn't feel too forced with the 'arty' questions written on place mats?

Is the neglected internal courtyard in the Andrew Duncan Clinic an interesting proposal for you?
All the best
Anne

20 May 2004. Excerpt from diary:

Through speaking to Sue, staff, patients and the other trainees, I suggest film could be the best way to explore issues of self-harm as it can easily be shown in an art or healthcare context. Sue thought that more people would benefit from the development of the A.D.C. courtyard, whereas only a few people would benefit from seeing the film on training days.

Lunch 14 July 2004, 12.30–2.30pm. Excerpt from diary:

Sue and I begin to look at other artists who have dealt with issues of mental health in their video work. Performance artist Bobby Baker's How to Live (looks at training video methods used in cognitive behavioural therapy), Suicide Box by the Bureau of Inverse Technology, Caz McIntee's Man's Search for Happiness and Top Spot by Tracey Emin.

From: Sue Robertson
Date: 25 November 2004 08:54:24
Subject: Bobby Baker's article ...

Hi Anne
Received & read the above this am - didn't fully grasp it at first (my non-creative head) but was then fascinated by Bobby's unique thinking & take on ordinary things - much food for thought!
Have a good weekend!
Sx

Sunday 12 December 2004. Excerpt from diary:

I met with Bobby Baker. I asked her to be a consultant on the ...and the trainees project. Bobby agreed to visit the Royal Edinburgh in spring 2005 when we would screen her DVD How to Live to a small invited audience and then follow this with a discussion (over food!).

Lunch 8 April 2005. Excerpt from diary:

Food: Delia's roasted vegetables (with fennel), couscous and a harissa sauce.
Attending: guest Dr Jane Morris (consultant psychiatrist, young persons unit, and leader of the South of Scotland Cognitive Behavioural Therapy Group) plus Sue and Anne.
Bobby can't attend but we still screen her DVD 'How to Live' (50mins, colour, sound, 2005).

From: Jane Morris
Subject: Re: Bobby Baker video
Date: 12 April 2005 12:46:36

Dear Anne Elliot,
Thank you so much for the delicious lunch and the chance to meet with you and Sue.
I did enjoy having the chance to watch and discuss Bobby's video. It came across as affectionate mockery of the CBT therapy and made me think about the ways in which therapy is performance, while performance – for the audience as well as the actor – is therapy ...
Thanks once more
Jane

18 April 2005. Excerpt from diary:

Jane would like to screen Bobby's film at her C.B.T. group. I requested that I join the group for the screening. It has left me thinking where Sue and I can take our project. We are still meeting, having lunch and exchanging ideas and stories. The training between us continues as we work towards a visual outcome for our ideas.

Collaboration or Situation

Jan-Bert van den Berg

*That brings me back to this idea of concentric circles, by which
I mean art at the margins, that has not been quite absorbed into
the art-world mainstream. But I believe that these areas of art
become successive rings, absorbed into the whole, that enlarge
our understanding of what is art, and are not hot, new topics that
replace/displace each other.*
– Mary Jane Jacob [1]

There is no single right way of working. Different experiences and
expectations can shape exciting outcomes. They can also stifle
potential and create a tendency to play it safe. Taking risks should
be inherent to creative endeavour.

Artlink's work in hospitals over the years has led us to a strong
belief that experimentation is important; however, this comes with
responsibilities. The results need to be relevant to the experiences
of the hospital community.

The origins of our particular collaborative approach can be found in
the Fusion Project [2], in which we commissioned artists to make art
for Lothian hospitals and also set up collaborations between artists
and patients. Artlink tried not to anticipate specific results from
these collaborations: instead, we listened and observed. The artists
and patients spent time getting to know one another, and the
artworks that resulted from these longer-term relationships were
stunning: they crossed a boundary.

The artworks that did not involve this level of collaboration
did not have the same depth. Although greatly enjoyed by the
departments and very professional in their execution, they lacked
something when you considered them alongside the collaborations.
This insight suggested that we might approach our work from a
different angle in any subsequent project.

Meaningful Arts Processes

Functionsuite was conceived in response to what we had learned from the Fusion Project, and we were also influenced by other artists and projects that have sought to involve communities in the production of artworks: WochenKlausur, Littoral, Suzanne Lacy, Mary Jane Jacobs and the Royston Road Project.[3] We wanted Functionsuite to have a flexible framework which would allow artistic direction to be determined by all those who took part: artist, patient, administrative staff, doctor or nurse. We wanted to create opportunities for artists and members of the hospital community to gain a mutual understanding of healthcare experiences. Equally, we sought to encourage working relationships which would lead to a greater understanding of art. We wanted to support meaningful artistic processes that resulted in shared artistic outcomes. And we wished to encourage the development of artistic strategies that would transform the hospital environment.

Understanding that a written proposal and the resulting practice can be quite different things, we entered new and almost uncharted territory! The approach represented a very different and intriguing way of working. Based within hospitals, Functionsuite gave artists unusual physical and intellectual environments in which to work. The first task was to create 'research' periods – opportunities for artists to learn from hospital staff and patients and to establish working partnerships. The second task was to shape and guide these partnerships towards the creation of an artwork. The third was to produce a publication discussing and analysing these processes. It was clear that responsibility for achieving all this would lie not only with the artists and the people within the hospitals, but also with those managing and realising the project. We knew we were aiming for an ideal that was possibly not achievable. We had embarked on a difficult journey. Of course, we learn most from difficulties.

Art is a convenient term for a mid-space location where you don't need cultural permission to carry out certain corrective tasks in relation to society in general. There are a number of keys to

understanding my work; one is distraction ... What I like about the position of an artist is that you might start out intending to be a DJ but end up cleaning the floor with vodka and glitter instead.
– Liam Gillick [4]

Work began by identifying hospital departments and individuals with an interest in being involved. We used existing contacts and created new ones through open discussions. The Functionsuite team, Anne Elliot, Kate Gray and Caz McIntee, sought artists whose arts practices would work well in the various emerging situations. This is how a dating agency works – introducing people into (hopefully) productive pairings. The job of the Functionsuite team was to broker these new relationships and thereby encourage a cross-fertilisation of ideas.

Changing and Challenging Expectations

Initially, the Functionsuite project aimed to create opportunities for artists to investigate particular areas of the healthcare environment. This included administrative as well as medical activities. Prepared to find indifference to any type of artistic activity, we instead discovered a hospital community that was incredibly open and welcoming. We encountered few people who were suspicious of the artists; we found plenty who were questioning. It is this challenge that builds good relationships.

Nothing focuses the mind more than having to explain your artwork or your intended artwork to someone who is unfamiliar with your jargon, your way of working and your expectations. It initiates a learning process requiring you to think about what you do from the point of view of another. It forces you to communicate clearly and simply, and it forces you to listen. Real success in Functionsuite occurs where the artists have listened well and have developed their ideas with the full involvement of their collaborators: where this hasn't happened, results have fallen short of their full potential.

This has raised questions about artists' abilities to listen, negotiate their expectations, and understand the differences between

themselves and other people. It has challenged us to look at how we facilitate artists and how we can create positive critical dialogue within a project. The Functionsuite team has become experienced in supporting artists. They have listened and discussed and occasionally concluded that an idea could go no further.
When this happened, it was neither destructive nor negative; it was our learning curve. It shaped our understanding of our aims and what was possible. In many instances, the Functionsuite team helped the artists to refocus and seek out more contact with their collaborators.

Collaboration and Reciprocation

Our aim has been to support artistic processes in which the results are owned jointly by the artists and their collaborators. We are not interested in the artist simply reflecting and reinterpreting the other person's experience – an approach often used by artists working in public settings. We want artists to go deeper and search out a real common purpose, in order to create something with a shared relevance. It is more about reciprocation and synergy, and the discovery of a shared interest, common experience or heart-felt belief. Interestingly, a more experienced artist does not necessarily guarantee a more successful result: it comes down to a willingness to listen and compromise – something we all needed to learn.

Equal ownership is not necessarily a prerequisite of success. Often, the most interesting projects are those where ownership is unequal and there are positive tensions between artists and collaborators. 'Uncooperative' or 'critical' collaborators challenge the artist and the arts organisation's preconceptions of 'collaborative' or 'socially engaged' art. They provide a reminder of the real – the practical – and give grounding to the work we undertake.

How do we measure success? Do we look at what the artists, their collaborators and the organisations have learned? Or at the quality of the shared artistic outcomes? Or does success relate to the level of willingness of the artists, staff and patients to take risks, and how much thought they put into their participation?

Of course, it is all these things. Naturally, there is a tendency to highlight success and play down shortcomings. What didn't work so well? What fell short and didn't succeed? When things don't go as expected, you either have something quite special or you are in one of those cul-de-sacs where you admit defeat.

Failure often comes from insufficiently preparing the ground, a lack of clarity about intent, an inability to advance thinking, or from simply not listening. As organisers, we need to make sure that artists enter this environment fully prepared. This involves clearly establishing relationships with key contacts within the hospital community; setting a very clear brief about the aims of the activity; giving opportunities for discussion and critique of proposed approaches; and developing a shared understanding of what results or outcomes are expected.

Visibility and Experimentation

An issue that has cropped up occasionally is that of visibility. If a project's outcome is a process and a description of that process, rather than a tangible product, how does this benefit the wider hospital population? Does the hospital require concrete, material responses in order to discern a clear and certain benefit? Possibly, but what seems evident is that the hospital community is open to experimentation and risk-taking, and we should build on this!

How far did the Functionsuite project succeed in achieving its aims? Did it venture into realms so experimental that it lost the very people it sought to engage? Perhaps surprisingly, this has very rarely been the case, and it helped that some projects were halted at the research phase. But mostly the people with whom we worked made that leap and 'got stuck in', even when they thought it was a little weird or possibly a waste of time. Indeed, sometimes it seemed the artists found the required mind shifts more difficult than did their collaborators.

What follows Functionsuite needs to take precisely this into account: not the limitations of the environment or the assumed indifference or hostility to art in a healthcare setting, but the need for clearer support for the artists and constructive criticism of art within this context. ■

Endnotes

Is Collaboration the Cure? p. 16–51

1. Electroconvulsive Therapy, which involves placing electrodes on the temples, on one or both sides of the patient's head, and delivering a small electrical current. The aim is to produce a seizure lasting up to a minute, after which the brain activity should return to normal.

The Ideal Ward p. 26–33

1. Philippe Pinel (1745–1826) pioneered moral therapy in revolutionary Paris and supposedly struck off the chains from the patients at the Salpètriêre and Bicêtre asylums there.
2. Erving Goffman (1922–1982) defined the 'total institution' as 'a place of residence and work where a large number of like-situated individuals, cut off from the wider society for an appreciable period of time, together lead an enclosed, formally administered round of life' (Erving Goffman, introduction to Asylums: Essays on the Social Situation of Mental Patients and Other Inmates, Penguin edition, 1991).
3. Kingsley Hall, London (1965–1970), a therapeutic community where patients and doctors lived together under supposedly non-hierarchical rules, was set up by R.D. Laing, a Glaswegian psychoanalyst whose books, including The Divided Self (1960), are well known.
4. Irwin Altman, The Environment and Social Behavior: Privacy, Personal Space, Territory, Crowding (Brooks/Cole Pub. Co, 1975).

Delicate Territory p. 54–71

1. See, for example, Guy Debord, La Société du Spectacle (Buchet-Chastel, 1967)
2. www.muf.co.uk
3. Essential lines to doctors etc. were to be excluded.
4. The artists distributed flyers to everyone who was going to be called one month in advance of the project going live.

Collaborators and Artists in Conversation p. 72–87

1. The Royal Edinburgh Hospital is the psychiatric hospital in Morningside where Functionsuite is based. It is being replaced by a new hospital which is expected to open in 2008.
2. See p. 55–61.
3. Albert Nicolson, a main collaborator in the Mayday Pavilion project, is a former patient who has studied architecture and is interested in providing recreational opportunities for patients. He is current chairperson of the Patients' Council.
4. See p. 62–81.
5. Shona Ferguson, along with Sue Robertson, runs a weekly support group in the Church Centre for people who hear voices, or have experienced hearing voices.
6. Caz McIntee, Functionsuite programme manager
7. See p. 26–33
8. See p. 82–90

Lines of Resistance to Human Misery p. 88–105

1. Italo Calvino, 'Afterword: The Four Paths of Primo Levi', in Primo Levi, The Search for Roots (Allen Lane, The Penguin Press, 2001).
2. Private Finance Initiative is one of a range of government policies designed to increase private sector involvement in the provision of public services. PFI entails transferring the risks associated with public service projects to the private sector in part or in full.
3. 'Cooperative work' is a term that Jeanette Bell herself introduced during her earlier collaborative projects.

The 'C' word p. 106–131

1. www.roystonroadproject.org
2. Francis McKee, 'Free Style', in My Father is the Wise Man of the Village (Artlink & The Fruitmarket Gallery, 2002), p. 37, a book about Fusion, a previous Artlink hospital project.
3. Mary Jane Jacob, Practicing in Public, www.communityarts.net/readingroom/archivefiles/2003/10/practicing_in_p.php.
4. Artlink had developed these relationships and this awareness through the Fusion project, see note 2.

5. She was pregnant with twins.
6. The Timeline, www.mdx.ac.uk/www/study/mhhtim.htm, is a mental health history that includes information about asylums and community care, with links to Andrew Roberts's book on the Lunacy Commission (2004) and other mental health writings and resources.
7. Mary Jane Jacob, Practicing in Public.

Unchain the Lunatics: two stories p. 115–119

1. The title is taken from the Mental Health History Timeline by Andrew Roberts, www.mdx.ac.uk/www/study/mhhtim.htm#Pinel.
2. Extract from a letter to Anna Best from Gemma Nesbitt, 2004.
3. Andrew Roberts, Mental Health History Timeline, www.mdx.ac.uk/www/study/mhhtim.htm, Middlesex University, 1981. Phrases from this website appear throughout Unchain the Lunatics: two stories, with the kind permission of Andrew Roberts.
4. A social anthropologist involved in the Functionsuite projects. See his essay on p. 16–117.
5. One of the two core Functionsuite artists.
6. Gemma Nesbitt wrote one letter, too, which is quoted in Unchain the Lunatics: two stories.

...and the trainees p. 120–131

1. Anna Best, artist, see p. 115–119

Collaboration or Situation p. 132–137

1. Mary Jane Jacob, quoted in Carole Tormollan, 'Concentric Circles: An Interview with Mary Jane Jacob', High Performance, 69/70 (Spring/Summer 1995).
2. A 3-year programme of work in Lothian hospitals: see My Father was the Wise Man of the Village (Artlink & The Fruitmarket Gallery, 2002), a publication that accompanied an exhibition about the Fusion Project.
3. www.wochenklausur.at; www.littoral.org.uk; www.roystonroadproject.org
4. Liam Gillick, quoted in Claudia Schmuckli, projects 79 liam gillick: literally (The Museum of Modern Art, New York, 2003).

Country's Good at Speed Front and back inside covers

A one-to-one collaboration resulting in a series of sculptures inspired by the design of electronic musical instruments and modernist church architecture.

Royal Edinburgh Hospital and Glasgow Sculpture Studios
December 2004–April 2005

James Mclardy, artist
Lewis Aarrestad, ex-patient

A Paper Marriage p. 9–16

A video installation about bees and beekeeping was created and shown at the hospital, bringing the private pastime of a member of the hospital staff into the public realm of the hospital.

Western General Hospital
January 2004–November 2005

Anne Elliot, core Functionsuite artist
Dr David Wright, consultant anaesthetist in the intensive care unit at the Western General Hospital (until his retirement in April 2005)
&
Bron Wright, David Wright's partner. Together they won the 2004 and 2005 Scottish Beekeepers' Association Trophy at the Royal Highland Show, Edinburgh.

Mimic Me p. 17–25

A film of improvised acting in which professional actors mimic a patient and an artist.

Royal Edinburgh Hospital
June 2003–July 2005

Anne Elliot, core Functionsuite artist
Stewart Murray, patient
&
Morna Burdon, actor
Sean Hay, actor
Alan Currall, artist and project consultant

The Ideal Ward p. 26–33

A focus group, comprising hospital users and staff, drew up a brief for an ideal ward in a psychiatric hospital. The project was inspired by current plans to rebuild the Royal Edinburgh Hospital.

Royal Edinburgh Hospital
January 2004–March 2005

Steve Duval, artist
Susan Tennyson, commissioning nurse for the new Royal Edinburgh Hospital
Ruth Rooney, project worker Patients' Council, Royal Edinburgh Hospital
Robert Taylor, Kim McLauchlan and Gwen, ex-patients

The New Republic p. 34–41

A children's utopia built in a courtyard overlooked by a children's ward.

St John's Hospital
January 2004–June 2005

Paul Carter, artist
Erin Kirsop, Rebecca Kirsop, Sophie Livingstone, Simon McHarg, Claire Weir and Kirsty Weir, patients at the children's ward
Lynn Haddow, ward charge nurse
Janice Hawthorn, play leader
Mary Benson, play coordinator
&
Beth Cross, storyteller from the Appleseed Storytelling Project

Untold Tales of the Unexpected p. 42–54

A research project which looked at how people describe epilepsy or seizures. Epilepsy was also explored as a metaphor for feelings of loss of control within culture.

Western General Hospital
January 2004–May 2005

Kate Gray, core Functionsuite artist
Dr Adam Zeman, consultant neurologist, Western General Hospital
Enlighten and other epilepsy support groups in Edinburgh and the Lothians
&
Justin Kenrick, social anthropologist
Maureen Sangster, poet, volunteer and ex-patient at Royal Edinburgh Hospital

Mayday Pavilion p. 57–63

A temporary structure in the grounds of Royal Edinburgh Hospital made from recycled non-clinical hospital waste. The pavilion housed a programme of activities over the May bank holiday weekend.

Royal Edinburgh Hospital
January 2004–May 2005

Kate Gray, core Functionsuite artist
Albert Nicolson, Patients' Council at Royal Edinburgh Hospital
&
Paul Barham, architect
The Talamh Life Centre
Artlink volunteers

ARoundhead p. 64–81

An automated telephone system at Royal Edinburgh Hospital. Phone calls from Oliver Cromwell encouraged staff to pass around messages, songs, jokes and rude noises.

Royal Edinburgh Hospital
January 2004–June 2005

Graham Harwood and Richard Wright of Mongrel, artists
Tom Arnott, facilities manager
Louise Birrell, assistant facilities manager
Gill Watson, project coordinator
Teresa Quinn, telephone switchboard manager
&
Matthew Fuller, Francesca da Rimini, script researchers
David Griffiths, script workshop leader
Neil Conrich, actor, voice of Oliver Cromwell
Mary Mullen, sound production

The Crime of Uglyfication

A script for a short courtroom drama that was videoed and then premiered at the Cameo cinema, Edinburgh, in March 2005.

Royal Edinburgh Hospital
November 2004–March 2005

Michelle Naismith, artist
Jeanette Bell, artist and patient

Stories from the A&E

Looked at the different tactics people use to cope with working in the high stress environment of the accident and emergency department. Events and conversations culminated in an installation of photography and text.

Royal Infirmary of Edinburgh
June 2002–June 2005

Ilana Halperin, artist
Dennis Purcell, nurse practitioner
&
Other staff from the A&E department

A Knitting Bee p. 98–106

A blanket was knitted and then taken into the Scottish landscape to be photographed. An exhibition of this work at the hospital gave rise to a series of very sociable knitting bees.

Royal Edinburgh Hospital
June 2003–April 2005

Anne Elliot, core Functionsuite artist
Jeanette Bell, artist and patient
Margaret Dickson, cousin of Jeanette Bell
Margaret McIntyre, retired pathologist and member of Western General Hospital's Arts Committee
Margaret Watson, friend of Margaret McIntyre
&
Other knitting bee participants

The Comic Project p. 107–114

Drawings of the hospital sterilisation & decontamination unit at the Royal Infirmary.

Royal Infirmary of Edinburgh
February 2004–April 2005

Mick Peter, artist
Gordon Dickson, sterilisation technician
&
Garry Gorham, HSDU manager

Unchain the Lunatics: two stories

A fictional text about confinement and asylums.

St John's Hospital and Royal Edinburgh Hospital
November 2003–May 2005

Anna Best, artist
Dominic O'Donnell, patient
Gemma Nesbitt, nursing home resident
&
Neil Chapman, artist and project consultant

... and the trainees

Monthly luncheons with invited guests from the artistic and hospital communities. The meals created time and space in which to share personal and professional experiences and discuss artistic, social and political ideas.

Royal Edinburgh Hospital
November 2003–June 2005

Anne Elliot, core Functionsuite artist
Sue Robertson, clinical development nurse

Acknowledgments

Collaborators & Contributors

Lewis Aarrestad
Andrew Anderson
Tom Arnott
Wendy Arthur
Paul Barham
Bobby Baker
Ruth Barr
James Batchen
Jeanette Bell
Dr Jeanne Bell
Mary Benson
Dr Best
Matthew Best
Jon Bewley
Alison Bonney
Hazel Britain
Morna Burdon
Robin Burley
Lorna Carigan
Neil Chapman
Anna Chihofska
Gillian Christie
Neil Conrich
Andrea Crociani
Beth Cross
Alan Currall
Chris Dennis
Gordon Dickson
Margaret Dickson
Neil Dinse
Jackie Drummond
Mike Duncan
Shona Ferguson
Liza Fior
Dr Maia Forrester
Matthew Fuller
Garry Gorham

David Griffiths
Gwen
Lynn Haddow
Harriet Harris
Sarah Harvey
Janice Hawthorn
Sean Hay
Dr James Hendry
Louise Holden
Sandy Hurry
Moira Jeffery
Lucy Kimbell
Erin Kirsop
Rebecca Kirsop
Angela Lamb
Miss Lawson
Sophie Livingstone
Jamie Macdonald
Simon McHarg
Margaret McIntyre
Kim McLauchlan
Jim McLaughlan
Kathleen McLeish
Rebecca Marr
Jackie Meikle
Moodle Pozart
Bill Mooney
Abi Mordin
Dr Jane Morris
Stewart Murray
Gemma Nesbitt
Ant Nicol
Albert Nicolson
Michael O'Dare
Dominic O'Donnell
Jenny Olley
Yvonne Paton

Merrick Pope
Dennis Purcell
Teresa Quinn
Florian Quistrebert
Iain Reid
Lesley-Jean Rigg
Francesca da Rimini
Andrew Roberts
Sue Robertson
Paul Rooney
Ruth Rooney
Maureen Sangster
Jim Shanks
Becky Shaw
Claire Smith
Dr David Steadman
Calum Stirling
Dr Jon Stone
Norman Swan
Talamh Life Centre
Robert Taylor
Susan Tennyson
The Ladies Art Group
Beth Thompson
George Vint
Zoe Walker
Bill Wallace
Gill Watson
Margaret Watson
Claire Weir
Kirsty Weir
Dr David Wright
Bron Wright
Matsuko Yokokoji
Dr Adam Zeman

Artists

Anna Best
Paul Carter
Adam Chodzko
Steve Duval
Ilana Halperin
Graham Harwood
James Mclardy
Rachel Mimiec
Michelle Naismith
Mick Peter
Sarah Tripp
Richard Wright

Volunteers

Erica Burberry
Val Cannon
Sarah Cameron
Gerard Doherty
Emma Duncan
Emily Farncombe
Arek Kozak
Derek Sutherland
Tessa Welsh

Technical Assistance

Malcolm Hosie
Ross Ingleston
Jordan Karr-Morse
Mary Mullen
Ewan Robertson
Christopher Walker

Invited Writers

Dr David Wright, retired consultant anaesthetist
Justin Kenrick. social anthropologist
Magnus Linklater, journalist
John Beagles, artist and writer

Functionsuite Team

Anne Elliot, artist team leader
Kate Gray, senior artist
Caz McIntee, programme manager

Supported by:

Charlotte Collingwood, gallery manager
Justin Kenrick, researcher
Angela Kingston, managing editor
Kirsty Macdonald, acting gallery manager

Artlink

Jan-Bert van den Berg, director
Alison Stirling, projects director
Vanessa Cameron, administrative coordinator
Alison Thorburn, bookkeeper
Kara Christine, route-map coordinator
Kate Stancliffe, administrative assistant

Lothian Hospital Arts Consortium

Terry Griffiths, St John's Hospital
Sally Tucker, St John's Hospital
Louise Birrell, Royal Edinburgh Hospital
Dr Andrew Elder, Western General Hospital
Dr David Wright, Western General Hospital
Dr Ian Laing, Royal Infirmary of Edinburgh
Sandy Young, Royal Infirmary of Edinburgh

Colophon

Edited by Angela Kingston, Jan-Bert van den Berg and the
Functionsuite team: Anne Elliot, Kate Gray and Caz McIntee.
Copy editing and editing of the discussion by Hazel Mills
Transcription and additional sub-editing by Elizabeth LeMoine

All photographs by Anne Elliot apart from:
Jeanette Bell p. 74
Paul Carter p. 34, 35, 37
Charlotte Collingwood p. 85
Alan Dimmick p. 1, 33, 38, 51, 52, 68, 70, 75, 90
Kate Gray p. 22, 39, 41– 44, 80, 84
Ilana Halperin p. 69, 71, 72
Arek Kozak p. 2
Caz McIntee p. 55, 56, 58, 59
Stephen Robinson p. 67
Christine Stewart p. 12
Alison Stirling: drawing of Oliver Cromwell's death mask p. 69
David Wright: bee image for cover and p. 13

Designed by Mark Beever
Printed by BAS Printers
Published by Artlink Edinburgh & the Lothians, 2005
ISBN: 0 9551882 0 2
   978 0 9551882 0 6

Artlink
13a Spittal Street
Edinburgh
EH3 9DY
T 0131 229 3555
F 0131 228 5257
E info@artlinkedinburgh.co.uk
www.artlinkedinburgh.co.uk

www.functionsuite.com
Functionsuite website design by 16k design works

Functionsuite was funded by Lothian NHS Board Endowment Fund and Scottish Arts Council Lottery Fund with additional assistance from The Law Department of Edinburgh University, Loxley Colour, The Church Centre and Edinburgh Voluntary Organisations Council.

LOTHIAN HOSPITAL ARTS CONSORTIUM

Scottish Arts Council LOTTERY FUNDED

NHS Lothian

Back inside cover:
Project: Country's Good at Speed
Lewis Aarrestad and James Mclardy's finished work on display at the Glasgow Sculpture Studios.